PIECES FOR PROFIT

How High Performing Organizations Maximize Profitability to Achieve Greater Success

Feel free to contact David at
info@unique-solutionsinc.com, or more information can
be accessed at **www.strategypeoplecustomers.com**
or **www.unique-solutionsinc.com**.

David Yeghiaian

PIECES FOR PROFIT

How High Performing Organizations Maximize Profitability to Achieve Greater Success

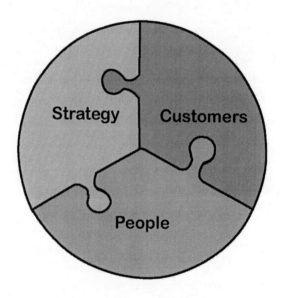

David Yeghiaian

Winners Success Network Publishing
Neenah, Wisconsin

PIECES FOR PROFIT by David Yeghiaian

First edition, first printing
Copyright © David Yeghiaian, 2007
All rights reserved

ISBN: 09666819-7-5

Published by Winners Success Network Publishing
P.O. Box 404
Neenah, WI 54957-0404

Printed in the United States of America
Cover designed by Lung Yang and Arketype Inc.
Graphics designed by Lung Yang

This book is dedicated to my wife, my best friend and my life partner, Kim. She has helped me become the person I am today.

Contents

Acknowledgements

There are many acknowledgements due when a book represents more than 15 years of experience, research, thoughts, observations and discussions. Because this book reflects years of work, it is impossible to name and appropriately express my appreciation to all the individuals who have helped. I will do my best to express thanks to those that have made the most impact.

In terms of experience, I would like to thank the organizations which have chosen to offer me a position. This provided me with an initial scope of experience and learnings. The learnings include knowledge, skills and competencies; as well as being a better leader and person. Those I have learned from include Barclay Fitzpatrick, Bob Smith, Dean Freeman, my Falk Corporation team, David Pozniak, Mike Haddad, Steve Shelley, Ron Dunford, Claudio Diaz and Gunnar Scholer.

Academically, a large gratitude goes to Don McCartney for being a friend, teacher, colleague and reviewer. In addition, I also owe a great deal of thanks to the numerous students I have had the privilege to learn from and teach. I have learned as much from many of them as I hope they have been able to learn from me.

Jason Jennings made a much larger impact on me than he may ever know. Upon meeting this famous author and speaker, he was genuine and friendly. Years ago, he signed one of his books and wrote, "to a bright guy… you got a future (your mind proves it)." This gave me the kick in the butt to begin thinking about writing this book.

Lung Yang was vital to the book cover and graphics throughout. His responsiveness and assistance are remarkable. He is also a former student and someone I am glad to call a friend. Arketype Inc. was instrumental in the final cover design, and I am thankful to know such as high-concept creative agency.

Mike Scott taught me how to write as my high school teacher and Don Gore helped improve my writing more as my college instructor. Rory Gillespie helped take it to another level as a former leader.

As a business owner, I have been lucky to have learned from so many other successful leaders. This includes Tim Weyenberg, Karl Schmidt, Lou LeCalsey, Dan Johnson, Tony Cerato, Brian Kult, Jeff Plitt and Damian LaCroix; as well as friends Mark Harris, Frank Campenni, Jeff Gahnz, Ray Faccio, Jim Rivett, Syed Akhter and Marianne Oates.

This book would not have been achieved without many prior and current team members such as Megan Rushmer, Kristin Herbst and Ryan Price. I have been fortunate to have Laure Cisler as a team member as her editing skills and attention to detail made this book possible. Marc Kostac has been extraordinary for his insights, friendship and dedication. As someone once told me, Marc represents a good "yin" to my "yang" and his thought-provoking questions and analysis have made this book a much better resource.

Finally, I would like to thank the organizations and leaders that have allowed me to interact with them, as well as each of you reading this book. Without you, none of this would be possible. I hope you enjoy the book.

Introduction

"Dream as if you'll live forever. Live as if you'll die today."
– James Dean

This is a book about Strategy, People and Customers. It is geared toward you. If you're reading this book, you want your organization to achieve greater success by maximizing profitability and/or you simply want to continuously learn.

Please note some key words used in this book:

- **You**: The reader. This book is targeted for business leaders and/or business individuals, as well as collegians.
- **I**: David Yeghiaian. The author who has created the organizational approach discussed in this book. The approach – Strategy, People and Customers – is based on personal experiences, observations, research and analysis.
- **We/Our**: As president and owner of a strategic business advising firm, Unique Business Solutions, most references pertain to examples where the firm – or I personally – have partnered with clients or business leaders.

Several years ago, I attended Franklin Covey's "7 Habits of Highly Effective People" workshop. If you have ever read Stephen Covey's book on this topic or attended the workshop, you know a key item is to write a personal mission statement. This is something I took seriously and continually thought about and worked on for several weeks after the workshop ended.

The result led to the creation of my own firm. Its main objective is my personal mission and passion: to help others (organizations and people) continuously improve by becoming more productive and successful.

Based on this, I was determined to "practice what I preach" and began reflecting on one question: **How can organizations become more profitable and successful?**

For more than 15 years, I have partnered with and observed hundreds of organizations and thousands of business professionals across many industries. Based on these experiences, I developed an effective organizational model, tested across these industries, with consistent success.

The model includes three elements – Strategy, People and Customers. While there are other books and research supporting each of these – Strategy, People and Customers – separately, I do not believe there are any portraying them together as a puzzle. This book provides you with a vision of how the three work interdependently to help you continuously improve by becoming more profitable and successful.

The analyses, experiences and examples illustrate their inter-relationship. I use the term puzzle, because as you solve a puzzle, you begin with those pieces that make the most sense to you. While this organizational model has only three pieces – Strategy, People and Customers – like a puzzle, all pieces need to fit together to maximize your productivity and profitability. Which piece you begin with may not matter as much as completing the puzzle.

This is a rather simple analogy; however, when a puzzle is incomplete, it is not very valuable. I will focus on each of the three pieces – Strategy, People and Customers – in more detail throughout this book. While Strategy and Customers are fairly self-explanatory, People merits a definition. I define People in the context of your employees. As each organization defines this differently – employees, associates, partners, team members, workers, human capital or labor – I chose the broad term People.

The individual items have been discussed historically, and more recently in popular books by Jason Jennings[1] and Jim Collins[2]. While many of you may have already read about one or two of these seemingly basic business principles, this is an opportunity to view all three together. As often as strategy, people and customers come up; in the 15+ years worth of discussions I have had with leaders, taken together, these items are not being completely acknowledged and thoroughly implemented by many organizations.

The puzzle – Strategy, People and Customers – relates to organizations of all sizes. Small, medium and large companies can become more profitable and successful when using these three puzzle pieces together. This includes 1-person start-ups, $10 million companies, $200 million organizations and Fortune 500 firms.

In Action

This book is divided into three sections. Section I discusses Strategy, Section II relates to People and Section III conveys Customers. The Epilogue brings all three together using an example of an acquisition and integration. Within each of the three sections, you will notice headings called "Strategy In Action," "People In Action" and "Customers In Action." Each relates to real life examples.

Strategy

Strategy in business exists to maximize productivity and profitability. As simple as it sounds, it is no simple task. Maximizing implies productivity and profitability must be performed to their highest levels. Maximum productivity and profitability are integral to the livelihood of your organization. Research shows that only 11 percent of executives strongly believe strategic planning is worth the effort.[3] We feel 11 percent is not nearly as high as it should be in placing emphasis on the creation and implementation of strategy.

Section I provides a concise working definition of strategy and allows you to begin to implement one. While people and customers, two pieces of our puzzle, are part of your strategy, they deserve unique consideration as separate entities. Our research indicates these are larger issues because of the unique co-dependent nature of the two.

People

An engaged employee is one that does meaningful work that they *and* the organization value. Research has shown that 93 percent of engaged employees would be willing to work for less money.[4] Having employees work for less pay should not be your main Human Resources task. This raises the question: "Does your organization consistently recruit and retrain engaged people?" Regardless of compensation, is the work your employees value the same work you value?

The climate in which work is equally valuable begins with a clear message from senior leadership to department leaders to middle-managers, and ultimately to the line workers. A strategy, with input across departmental lines and without overdependence on hierarchy, is preferred.

You'll be introduced to a new process called AL^2A^{SM} – Ask, Listen, Learn and Act.[5] This process relates to people and customers. Related to people, it includes gaining a detailed understanding of your people and their engagement in the organization. Employees shown to be emotionally engaged are typically more productive. Higher employee productivity transfers to more customers, and customers

> You'll be introduced to a new process called AL^2A^{SM} – Ask, Listen, Learn and Act.

receiving better service. This equates to higher customer satisfaction and loyalty, resulting in positive retention and increased revenues.

Customers

Similar to your people, the importance of truly identifying your customers' needs is explored. Engagement refers to the deep understanding your organization shares with its people, and the advantages in fostering this partnership. A partnership with similar possibilities exists for you and your customers. Your closest customers, those with an emotional connection to your organization, are fully engaged. These dedicated customers "provide a 23 percent premium to the organization's bottom."[6] Once these customers are connected to your organization, particularly *emotionally* connected, your partnership with them becomes truly beneficial. "Emotionally satisfied customers increased their spending by 67 percent over 12 months vs. only 8 percent by those not emotionally satisfied."[7]

By using AL^2A to obtain information on exactly what your customers need, you develop a partnership that truly involves catering to their main objectives. Prioritize your customers' main

objectives, and develop a partnership that makes profit a by-product
of that partnership. Asking some simple questions is the best way to start an AL^2A
dialogue. How do your customers decide what to purchase? What
products and services do they want? What post-sale interactions do
they require? You will be introduced to a process to effectively
understand your customers' needs.

Completing the Puzzle

An organization's people will ultimately affect customers, just as
customers will ultimately affect the people in it. If all people
elements of the organization are maximized (i.e., working in the right
positions to the best of their abilities), it affords the organization the
best chance to discover and retain customers. If customers are
providing maximum business to the organization, it provides the
organization the best chance to promote its employees. These two
pieces – people and customers – are important because of their
interdependence.

A high performing organization is ultimately trying to achieve its
maximum success. Like climbing a mountain, your organization
might have all the equipment it takes to reach the summit of success.
A creative marketing department, a reliable Human Resources
department, and a lean business culture are all equipment you need
to climb. However, without an experienced guide to help you know
how to use all of your equipment together (*Strategy, People and
Customers*), it is difficult to reach the top of the mountain. This book
will serve as a knowledgeable guide as you incorporate all your
equipment into a strategy for profitability and success.

Section I

Strategy

"Strategy is about making choices. The essence of strategy is choosing to perform activities differently than rivals do."
– Michael Porter

Strategy is defined as "a comprehensive view of all core elements of your organization that occur continuously with the benefit of maximizing productivity and profitability." One item to note in this definition is the word *all*. A strategy is most effective when it considers as many parts of the organization as possible, including the following:

* Customers
* Financials
* Operations and manufacturing
* People (Employees)
* Processes
* Products and services
* Research and development
* Technology

In effect, each functional area, department or division may have its own strategy puzzle. However, every organization may not operate each of these functional areas. While we will not discuss the individual segments of strategy, it is important to include each part of your organization in strategic planning to ensure a consistent message and alignment throughout the organization. We will discuss who is responsible for creating a strategy and how to relay the message throughout your organizational areas.

Strategy is defined as "a comprehensive view of all core elements of your organization that occur continuously with the benefit of maximizing productivity and profitability."

We also want to emphasize the word *core* in our definition of strategy. Research and experience show that an organization's people should focus on their strengths – what they do best – known as core competencies. While there are many facets of business, you should focus on core elements, continuously enhance these, and widen your competitive edge. New core elements may arise over time; however, focusing on non-core elements causes organizations to lose focus. As you consider what a comprehensive view of all core elements of your organization actually entails, try not to panic. There is a way to approach each of these core elements, to prioritize their importance and begin to comprehensively strategize a plan to make each core element more productive and profitable.

A view of these core elements suggests looking beyond today's current agenda when creating your strategy. This adds to the complexity of formulating a strategy. It has to include all core elements of your organization, and not just right now – in the future as well. And not just tomorrow – one year, three years and 10 years in the future. This process is simplified by standardizing a strategic planning process. We will explore the concept of one main objective – the idea that summarizes the deepest beliefs of where your organization is going. The main objective will drive your strategy.

Why do you and your employees show up and work hard every day of the week? It sounds like a question with an obvious answer. If you had to pause to answer it, you probably don't have one main objective. This is different than a mission or vision. It is the single concept that directs your strategy.

By the time your strategy is complete, it will be a comprehensive view of all core elements of your organization. To get to that point, we need to start big, really big, with one main objective. This concept has been described as an aligning principle that is "authentic, and that fundamentally impacts the way business is done." It is near and dear to leaders' fundamental beliefs.[1] In turn, your strategy – and your people and customers – will fulfill this main objective.

Chapter 1

Aligning Your Strategy

*"Strategy is not the consequence of planning,
but the opposite: its starting point."*
– Henry Mintzberg

If only 11 percent of your colleagues believe strategic planning is worth the effort, you may consider joining the other 89 percent. By not having a comprehensive view of all aspects of their organization, the majority of business leaders are spending more time devising short-term plans and making fewer actual decisions. Without a clear strategy of where your organization is headed today, tomorrow and beyond; decision making becomes inefficient, and that means expensive. Another way to view this is to first determine <u>what</u> you need to do and then <u>how</u> you should do it.

Aligning Functional Areas

Strategy must be universal throughout your organization. Traditionally, functional areas, departments, divisions and business units are responsible for implementing their own planning ideas and subsequently executing their own tasks. Sales handles Marketing,

Supply Chain Management handles transportation and distribution – on down the line – and supposedly everyone knows their *job*. These planning ideas may be reported to senior leadership, although this does not create an organization-wide strategy. A disconnect exists if your people know their job (even execute it well) but their divisional goals are not aligned with the organization's main goals.

Organizational leaders, not necessarily functional area leaders, are responsible for standardizing main goals, and also standardizing the organization's planning process. A clear, top-down objective ensures consistency. A process for prioritizing that objective into each division aids its consistency. Varied processes for planning and aligning priorities in divisions create inconsistency and process waste – two enemies of profitability and success.

An inconsistent strategic process, and inconsistent strategies, set up some divisions for differing levels of success. There is value to having equally productive or successful divisions. Consider great sales and an unproductive production and operations area. Unfilled orders are costly, just as shelves full of manufactured and unsold product are equally costly. A consistent strategic process provides functional areas with knowledge of how they align with other areas to fulfill the objective.

Functional areas contribute to determining the main objective and creating the strategy, then implementing and executing it. Consistent coordination and collaboration in planning ensures divisions know their responsibilities in the process. Process consistency ensures certain divisions do not dominate the process and steer the strategy favorably for their division. Imagine a disproportionately represented Human Resources department deciding the strategic direction of the company. Their goal is to increase staff by 20 people over the next three years. If the best practice adage is true, that revenue should increase by $300,000 for each employee added, is Sales aware they must now generate an additional $6 million?

A clear process of engaging all functional areas and secondary leadership levels is necessary for success. Gaining a clear understanding of the present situation and what your organization needs to do to create the strategy is a natural starting point.

Divisions or Intervisions

Your functional areas all operate within the confines of your organization. As People is being used to define employees, etc.; thus far, functional areas has been used to define divisions, etc. What about *external divisions*, or partners/suppliers with your organization? Similar to internal divisions, partner/supplier involvement ensures the same type of consistency in understanding objectives. Allowing your steadiest suppliers access to your objective and alignment across your value chain is sensible for forecasting. The same is true with other partners that will be affected by your strategy. Your emotionally connected partners will appreciate knowing their role with the future of your organization.

Toyota and Honda have adopted the idea of partner alignment. Japanese companies build "a close-knit network of vendors that continuously learn, improve and prosper, along with their parent companies." They have built this with North American auto suppliers. Toyota and Honda believe in sharing information in a structured method. Annually, Honda holds a strategic planning session with suppliers. The Japanese philosophy of strategic plan sharing is a testament to emotionally connecting with their partners; and their auto market leadership speaks to its success.[1]

Alignment of functional areas is a key outcome of strategic planning. Divisions lacking a shared view of the organization's ultimate goals are more likely to take on their own agenda. Consider the word *division*: "di-vision." The Latin prefix "di" literally means *apart*. So, unless you plan to prevent it, your *divisions* are "visions apart." We will introduce a new term, **_intervision_**, to identify your distinct functional areas. To align the functional areas completely, think of your unique functional areas as "intervisions" or "visions together." Your intervisions work cohesively sharing the same vision; with the strategy as the means and the objective as the end.

Aligning a shared objective, strategies and goals prevent the dreaded silo effect from occurring. Though divisions might be fulfilling their own agenda, no project is completed in one functional area. Problems begin to occur when work is handed-off. When Operations is complete and transportation is in the hands of Supply Chain Management, a hand-off occurs. When the product is delivered and responsibility is in the hands of Customer Service, another hand-off occurs.

These silos may operate well independently, yet are not accountable to the next silo over. This becomes increasingly complex in the context of an acquisition and integration, which will be discussed in the Epilogue.

> To align the functional areas completely, think of your unique functional areas as "intervisions" or "visions together." Your intervisions work cohesively sharing the same vision; with the strategy as the means to the objective as the end.

If functional areas are not aligned by a consistent main objective, what is the ultimate purpose of their actions? If Supply Chain Management's purpose is to deliver product at the lowest cost, and Customer Service's purpose is to deliver the product the fastest way possible. We are not aware of any company that accommodates both of those requests simultaneously. The opposing objectives of the two divisions in this example are evidence of a lack of a shared main objective. A shared main objective is the product of a shared view. Once accomplished, divisions, departments and/or functional areas become intervisions.

Aligning intervisions in the strategic process is a benefit as it gets people engaged in the same discussions to help determine the present situation. Without determining where you are currently, it is not possible to establish what you need to do next.

Determining the Present Situation

Determining your present situation involves all intervisions and providing information about what is currently happening. What items are being measured? How is the organization tracking against these measurements? What are the basic strengths, weaknesses, opportunities and threats? Where is the organization when viewing items such as operations, processes, employees, customers, finances?

This represents information intervisions bring to the beginning of a strategic session. The dialogue generated by the present situation naturally identifies gaps and areas to improve for the future. Although, how is future defined?

When planning the strategy for your organization's future, it is important to consider how far in advance to plan. Some companies have one-year strategic plans; while others have three-year, five-year, seven-year or even more lengthy plans. The year at hand – the approaching year – should be the core of your plan. And a three year strategy allows for the focus of the near future – the approaching year – and for a longer view. A three year strategy helps continually stay ahead of the market and competition.

Looking into the future involves internal factors affecting your organization; and includes external environment factors such as competition, economy, technology, politics, legislation, demographics, culture, or anything from the outside world affecting your organization.

Environmental forces create challenges and opportunities for your organization. Over the past few decades, America has seen increasing globalization as an example of opportunity and challenge for organizations of varying sizes and industries. Manufacturing has been faced with challenges such as competing with lower cost foreign labor and other factors.

Gaining an understanding of these items represents the first step in uncovering what you need to do.

Strategy In Action

A $50 million mechanical contracting firm questioned their own need for a strategic plan. More than 20 years after a three-party merger, this firm had been prospering from substantial revenue and organizational growth. The firm had expanded to seven divisions, each with a specialized technical competency, and added two regional offices.

This firm had attempted strategic planning by themselves. The problem was not writing a strategic plan; it was writing a quality plan, with clear goals. Additionally, the plan was seldom followed throughout the year. In previous strategic plans, no one was accountable for fulfilling items addressed in it. If the firm's revenues grew, everyone was happy. If they did not, no one looked back at the plan to see what went wrong. In effect, there was a process for writing a strategic plan without a process for implementing it.

Many organizations and leaders with high revenue and a differentiated service line would be delighted with this growth. However, this firm saw it as an opportunity to ask a key question: "Are we growing just for the sake of growing?" They then identified some issues the rapid growth had created:

- The formation of seven divisions had created a classic silo effect. There was little alignment between each of the divisions.
- Though the company had worked on strategy previously, people were never incorporated into the plan (except planning for turnover). There was no plan for employee retention and development of future leaders.
- Senior leadership was detached from the majority of the people in the organization. One senior leader said, "It is not my job to deal with personnel problems."

People were not only moving in different directions, they were unaware of the firm's main objective. Divisions were growing stronger, yet a lack of understanding of each other's concerns was negatively affecting morale.

Although growth had been positive, this firm needed to implement a comprehensive plan to strategically incorporate their people into the organization.

The president determined a different process for writing and implementing a strategic plan was needed, which in his mind included partnering with an external facilitator, among other things. Senior leadership also agreed to meet quarterly throughout the year for a continuous review. Quarterly is the least amount of time recommended to ensure the review of your plan is beneficial. Monthly or weekly is preferred based on company size, and many large companies have the ability to continuously review more frequently. Continuous review was especially important for this firm to make sure the time spent developing the plan was worthwhile.

Concluding Thoughts

Your strategic plan puts you in the driver's seat on the freeway of decision making. Your journey's objective is clear. Your strategy is the map. Roadblocks will appear on the way – competitors, unforeseen expenses and/or turnover. Turns will need to be made. With the direction of your organization set, each turn is a major decision on the journey to your ultimate objective.

Chapter 1: Summary

- Only 11 percent of leaders believe strategic planning is worth the effort.

- Strategy includes what you need to do and then how you should do it. The first step is to determine the present situation.

- To align the functional areas or divisions completely, think of your unique functional areas as "intervisions" or "visions together." Your intervisions work cohesively sharing the same vision; with the strategy as the means to the objective as the end.

- Include as many key stakeholders as possible when creating your strategy – intervisions, suppliers, key employees, etc.

- What did you learn from the Strategy In Action?

Chapter 2

Creating Creative Tension

*"Much strategy prevails over little strategy,
so those with no strategy cannot but be defeated."*
– Sun Tzu

Thus far, emphasis has been placed on aligning the intervisions in your organization and determining the present situation. The importance of an effective strategy is to completely satisfy people and customers – to ultimately become more productive and successful. We have not yet described how the main objective, the aligning force of your organization, is created. Before we do, it is necessary to differentiate the objective from a vision and mission.

Objective vs. Vision & Mission

Most organizations have vision and/or mission statements. In simplest terms, the vision defines where you want to go and the mission describes who you are and how you will achieve the vision. In our experiences, most organizations have vision and mission statements that are too long for employees to remember. This makes them irrelevant as few in the organization understand or care what they represent.

Even in instances where organizations have shorter statements, we have found few employees that can actually recite these or understand them. A main objective more clearly represents a mission than vision as it is short, concise and emotionally engaging for employees.

The main objective drives the process. It should not be reached haphazardly. In fact, the following five characteristics are suggested for any main objective:

1. The main objective should be grounded in the reality of the organization's present situation.

Essentially, the main objective must be realistically attainable and believable. Focusing on an objective so far removed from present reality makes the entire process worthless for all involved. This relates to financial information as your objective should not include financials because this is not a "rallying cry" for employees.

Strategy In Action

The mechanical contracting firm discussed in Chapter 1 fell into a trap early. They chose to focus their objective on financials, an easy way to fall into unrealistic territory. Originally, the objective was to increase net profit by 5 percent annually over three years. This sounds modest at first; however, the more we learned, the more unrealistic it became.

First, we discovered the industry average in mechanical contracting is between 1.5 – 2 percent annual net profit growth. This ambitious organization originally planned to grow it at nearly three times the average and try to sustain that growth every year for three consecutive years.

Second, we learned that in the history of the company, dating back to the 1920's, net profit had never increased by more than 1.7 percent annually. Now, we had proof that 5 percent was an unrealistic objective.

2. The main objective should facilitate creative tension for the organization.

The main objective should get people thinking differently, even in healthy opposition, to each other in order to create new ideas for accomplishing the objective. Simply, if the way things were previously done has not worked, a new approach is needed.

> The main objective should facilitate creative tension for your organization.

Strategy In Action

"Complete satisfaction is impossible." These were the words of the president of a global manufacturer of consumer products in the transportation industry. It was his belief that there is no such thing as complete satisfaction from a customer standpoint. The shortsightedness of his thinking is the fact that his consumer product carries a price tag of $250,000 to $1.5 million or more. Not to mention his competitors – who believed complete satisfaction is possible – were gaining market share.

Founded in the 1950's, this organization built a culture on customer service, not satisfaction. A culture built on customer service is not necessarily a bad thing, although if you need to provide a great deal of post-sales support, it indicates customers may not be completely satisfied. Senior leadership was going to need to change common thinking if an objective that stirred up creative tension was going to be found.

They did change. After 50+ years of believing complete satisfaction was impossible, the president vowed to make complete satisfaction a component of the main objective. Achieving this would be the cause for creative tension throughout the organization. What happened was certainly creative.

Though their consumer products were already the highest quality in the industry, it became apparent that a new standard would need to be set. The president himself even confessed he was physically too large to use the product his firm was designing, so a third-party was outsourced to work on redesign. A Quality Control expert was hired to ensure every aspect of the product was first rate – without defects.

These are simple steps that other firms may take for granted. Regardless, for a high performing company such as this, just doing what previously worked was not good enough. It was time to shake things up, develop an objective to do that, and generate some new ideas to create tension amidst the organization's people.

3. The main objective should be the result of the integrated thinking of the team, rather than a collection of individual objectives.

Engaging a broader group in your objective discussion fosters open dialogue and additional ideas. Individuals must place the organization and main objective before their own interests.

Strategy In Action

The mechanical contracting firm discussed in Chapter 1 nearly determined its main objective through a lone functional area's needs.

Referred to as a mechanical contracting firm, for simplicity's sake, the firm's engineering area did not feel properly represented in the strategic planning process. As it turns out, this organization is more than a mechanical contracting firm. Another core competency is performing engineering functions, as well as other contracting services. To properly represent the other functional areas in the strategic planning process, it was necessary to include members from each area in the leadership team to determine the main objective.

This firm now strives to be "an exemplary provider of mechanical contracting and engineering services, placing the needs of our customers and employees above all else." Acknowledging that engineering services are an important part of the strategic process is a big step to recognizing the potential of the entire organization to "place the needs of customers and employees above all else."

4. **The stakeholders – employees, customers and investors – must be able to see themselves or their interests represented.**

Why do we come to work every day? Why do we do business with you? Why do we invest in your company? You need to have understandable and believable answers to these questions.

Strategy In Action

A $3.5 billion global manufacturer in the food and beverage industry made sure its people's interests were represented in the main objective. This firm wanted its core values expressed in its objective, as has been previously recommended, anyone should.

The original objective involved a concept of *collaboration* between people, and there was no objection to collaboration between people in this organization. In fact, along with the strategy pieces previously discussed, it is recommended. However, after interviewing all key organizational stakeholders, the original objective had one critical flaw: the word *collaboration* was difficult for many people in the organization to comprehend. They felt they were engaged in *teamwork* – not collaboration.

The word teamwork was introduced into interviews and those involved found this word resonated with most people. Although people wanted to work with others, they just did not see this interest represented in the term *collaboration*. It was clear that teamwork was valued in the organization as the component that drives the strategy's objective. Eventually, a main objective was developed that focused on teamwork to match the organization's values.

5. The main objective should invite and inspire people to want to bring it to fruition.

In any organization, people identify with the objective. They must believe in fulfilling it, and if they do not, it is time for the individual to consider finding an organization that is more aligned with their interests.

The reasoning behind your objective is an interesting lesson in what your organization has valued in the past and how it transitions these values into the future. As we look at how the main objective fits into the strategic process, keep in mind this question: "Why do we come in to work every day?"

Strategy In Action

A national corporate training firm has a lofty objective: to never lay off a person. This objective appeals to the people of the organization and ensures they will want to see it come to fruition. Engaged people do not welcome lay-offs. They would rather be a part of a process they believe in, and work toward perfecting it.

Hidden in the objective of this organization is the by-product of the efforts to avoid layoffs. To maintain a compensation package, the organization must rely on revenue. Senior leadership must maintain and grow customer relations to provide its people steady employment. Upon closer examination, the desire to avoid lay-offs is a healthy incentive to maximize its productivity and profitability.

For this organization to engage its employees – to see its objective achieved – it must identify the core value that continuously motivates its people. Fortunately for this organization, its people have a value that transcends their jobs. Its people truly see themselves as more than corporate trainers. Rather, it is part of their personal spirit and beliefs that their training enlightens individuals to make people better through learning. This enlightenment will carry through to the trainer's respective client relationships.

Engaging People with Strategy

Strategy involves engaging the right people, in the right places, at the right time. Your well designed strategy will ultimately help you accomplish the main objective and you need to involve the optimum mix of people. The leadership team, essentially senior management, will drive the process. It is imperative to involve the rest of the company, particularly the next level of leadership. We will refer to this group as your next generation leaders. These individuals actually execute and implement the main items of your strategy, so their inclusion is important.

Along with this group, one key individual – an Executive Sponsor – is needed on the leadership team for each key goal in the strategy. This high-ranking person must believe in the strategic planning process because he/she will be the person ultimately accountable. The purpose of the Executive Sponsor is to be the sole person to say, "The buck stops here." This individual needs to promote the process, be hands on and become responsible for its success or failure.

The team generates the main objective so it flows through the organization. They have to brainstorm what your organization considers its core values. This team is obviously important in the initial development of the plan. Once the main objective is set, the team will discuss it with their intervisions to assist in devising the plan. This is addressed later in this chapter.

> Next generation leaders are those who actually execute and implement the main items of your strategy.

Continuous Review vs. Traditional Strategic Planning

Strategic decisions are the product of a well constructed strategic plan. These are high-impact decisions that significantly increase company profits. If decisions positively impact profits, the more decisions the better. Some believe that strategic decisions increase profits by 10 percent. Yet, as many as 89 percent of executives revert to another decision making approach, traditional decision making. Traditional decision making, the old fashioned way of strategic planning, is "typically an annual process and it is most often focused on individual business units."[1]

"How will our new product line be marketed this year?" A traditional question, answered with traditional decision making. This line of reasoning fails to consider a comprehensive view of other core elements of the organization besides marketing. It also allows for little strategic decision making beyond the start of the year (e.g., our new line this year). In one regard, traditional decision making is insular (it involves divisions, not intervisions) – and cumbersome (plan by plan for the entire year).

Traditional decision making is often a review and approve process. In traditional decision making, a functional area annually presents its best plan for the upcoming year to senior leadership, perhaps an executive committee. The plan might be good and well thought out, except for two major problems. First, it is time consuming for senior leadership to sit through presentation after presentation for each division on how it will achieve *its* own objectives. You may have guessed the second problem... if each functional area is presenting its own objectives and strategy for the coming year, how will each align?

With your organization aligned and heading for the main objective, your energy can be focused toward making strategic decisions that ultimately increase profits. We are no longer talking about day-to-day concerns based on divisions, rather strategic decisions serving as steps to promote the potential of your organization. With your time freed from "the grind," you are in a better position to improve the quality, expediency and quantity of decisions to be made.

Research has indicated that business leaders with no strategic plan make one strategic decision per year (see Graphic 2.1). Leaders focused on business units dependent on *annual* review make 2.5 strategic decisions per year. Those focused on issues through an *annual* review make 3.5 strategic decisions each year. Leaders using a *continuous* review process focused on business units make 4.1 strategic decisions throughout the year. However, leaders focused on issues with a strategy dependent on *continuous* review make an average of 6.1 strategic decisions per year. Those are impactful decisions that direct an organization.[2]

Graphic 2.1: Strategy Affecting Decisions[3]

Continuous Review	Continuous Review
Focused on issues	Focused on business units
6.1 DECISIONS PER YEAR	**4.1** DECISIONS PER YEAR
Annual Review	**Annual Review**
Focused on issues	Focused on business units
3.5 DECISIONS PER YEAR	**2.5** DECISIONS PER YEAR

The research indicates organizations engaged in a *continuous review* of their strategy, focusing on *issues*; make more decisions that actually drive the strategy and direction of the organization. The unpredictable nature of your environment makes strategy a continuous process. Strong leaders implement and execute a strategy. Strong *and* dynamic leaders recognize the changing world and adapt the plan to suit it.

Continuous Review Process

Once the strategy is determined and being implemented, it must be reviewed continuously. It is not to be thrown in the company archives with grandpa's first dollar earned. Reviewing the strategy is a continuous, preferably consistent, process. Your organization is constantly evolving. There is no reason why your strategy cannot evolve as well. A continuous review could mean weekly – pulling it out at leadership meetings – or at least monthly, and in the worst case, quarterly. A lot of time was invested creating the strategy, so it makes sense to review it as often as possible.

Your strategy is going to affect your corporate direction for the next year and beyond. Writing it at the optimal time, to hit the ground running, is critical for strategy implementation. The best time to prepare it is during the fourth quarter prior to the first year of its implementation, so it is ready to roll-out and communicate before quarter one of your fiscal year.

> Once the strategy is determined and being implemented, it must be reviewed continuously. It is not to be thrown in the company archives with grandpa's first dollar earned.

Depending on the size of your company, the strategic planning process may take as little as 1-3 days, or as long as several multiple-day meetings over four months. Plan off-site meetings. Use a non-traditional location to encourage innovative thinking. With the proper leadership team in place, create an environment fostering open-mindedness, opposed to traditional procedures used in the past.

An external facilitator can be a useful resource in the strategic planning process. If you have accepted the cost of your leadership team's time and an off-site location, it would be a shame if your strategy session lacked the necessary focus. A facilitator will help keep the process moving in the right direction and make sure everyone contributes.

Another key to continuous review is accountability. Ultimate accountability rests with the president. This individual is responsible for accomplishing all items in the strategy. Taken one step further, as the strategy is created, an individual should be accountable for each specific goal in the plan. This may be a mid-level person or top performer. This individual most likely reports to someone at a higher level, who reports to the president. Thus begins the flow of accountability from an individual to the president.

In any organization, the president or top leader undoubtedly commands respect. Because this process is crucial for the long-term success of your organization, the top leader must be committed to involvement. However, to gain everyone's opinions, it is best that the president keeps quiet during the onset to encourage contribution. Our experience has shown once a top leader begins to offer personal opinions, some creative synergies are lost. People may be hesitant to go against a top leader's viewpoint, for a variety of reasons, and that is not the purpose of this process.

A very active president had personally pioneered his firm's strategic planning process and was anxious to begin. One of his first questions was, "When can I talk?" He had to be settled down and informed that his people would get the first opportunity to present ideas in order to encourage an open dialogue. Unfortunately, his anxieties got the best of him, and he spoke up earlier than recommended. From that point on, people were hesitant to offer opinions opposed to his. Because he had spoken prematurely, discussions were stifled. He would have to allow his people the first opportunity to speak and offer ideas. From then on, only *after* all others had spoken did he offer his opinions. This provided buy-in and support from others. Remember, strategic planning is supposed to generate creative tension for your organization, not stifle it.

Goals

Previously, the concept of the main objective, how it is determined and what it should mean to your company, was introduced. The objective started as an organization-wide direction, derived by core values and distributed throughout the organization by senior leadership. Now, all intervisions have been introduced to it, and understand the objective, it is their turn to introduce benchmarks of their own – *goals* – specifically designed to fulfill the main organizational objective.

Senior leadership needs to initially develop these goals for each intervision. This provides a synergy between the organization-wide main objective and the goals at the intervision level. Intervisions can no longer say the main objective is too high-level or impractical for them. It has been clarified in terms specific for their area. Intervisions review the goals and provide feedback as they will be responsible for implementing the goals.

Using a main objective from a strategic business advising firm, let's develop one intervision's goal to fulfill it. The objective is "To help our people and clients continuously improve by becoming more productive and successful." Certainly, your Human Resources area needs to identify and position the right people to fulfill the objective. A goal for the Human Resources area might be: "We will provide the necessary training, career opportunities and compensation to attract, develop and retain the right people." A goal has been created to maintain the right people in the organization that will ultimately help fulfill the objective. Each of your intervisions needs a similar goal. Graphic 2.2 illustrates the Strategy Chain.

This begins with the main objective. The main objective flows to several goals. The goals are created for both your entire organization, as well as each intervision. Intervision goals are directly related to a respective organizational goal. Intervision goals are achieved through a series of strategies. Each strategy has a specific process owner within the intervision. The strategies are implemented through tactics – completed by individuals within the intervision.

In 1961, President Kennedy set a clear goal of becoming the first nation to successfully land on the moon by the end of the decade. The United States achieved this goal on July 20, 1969 when Apollo 11 landed on the moon. Like NASA, consider your goals. How long will it take to successfully achieve your goals? If a goal does not come together after year one, continue to work on it in year two and so on. By the time your strategy has culminated, each goal should be met (or modified during the continuous review process).

Graphic 2.2: The Strategy Chain

MAIN
OBJECTIVE

GOALS

STRATEGIES

TACTICS

SMART Strategy

It has been explained how your leadership team defines what your organization is all about. Leaders from each intervision have assisted in determining a main objective, and in turn, specific goals have been set for them to reach, for the purpose of meeting the main objective.

Strategic planning is an organization-wide process. Strategy touches everyone in an organization. The development of the strategy beyond this, at the tactical level, involves your next generation leaders – people closer to the fire.

Now, it is their turn to pay close attention to the main objective, and more precisely, goals that have been set for them. It is time for them to ask: "How will we meet this goal?" Had they already read this chapter, they would ask: "What are the strategies and tactics we will employ to meet this goal?"

Next generation leaders are those that have been identified as part of succession planning in key leadership roles. They are typically a few levels below the senior leadership team.

Planning at this level is (much more) Specific. Strategies at this level should be in Measurable terms. Strategies and tactics should be Attainable for achieving goals. Strategies should be Relevant in their ability to meet the goal. To assure they are on schedule, strategies should be Time-Based. If you have figured out the acronym we have spelled, then you, too, are SMART.

SMART strategies are Specific, Measurable, Attainable, Relevant and Time-Based. Using the previous Human Resources goal, an examination of a SMART process to meet this goal is helpful.

Main Objective: To help our people and our clients continuously improve by becoming more productive and successful.

Human Resources Goal: We will provide the necessary training, career opportunities and compensation to attract, develop and retain the right people.[4]

Now, a strategy to meet that goal:

"We will provide monthly coaching and mentoring sessions with all employees through the end of the year. These will be held on the second Monday of each month between 8 a.m. and noon through the end of the fiscal year." (Human Resources Manager – Ongoing Annually).

It is:

- **Specific** – The tactic is clearly stated in the goal of providing monthly coaching and mentoring sessions with all employees.
- **Measurable** – Since each employee is included on a monthly basis, this strategy can be measured for accuracy through the organization's performance management system (see Chapter 7 for more details).
- **Attainable** – The Human Resources Manager is noted for this strategy. This individual "owns" this respective goal, so he/she is ultimately accountable for its execution. As this goal relates to providing monthly coaching and mentoring with all employees, how can the Human Resources Manager attain this? To achieve the goal, this person must work with all other leaders to ensure they coach and mentor their own employees.
- **Relevant** – Coaching and mentoring are relevant parts of training.
- **Time-Based** – This strategy will be performed monthly until the end of the year.

This is a SMART process that your next generation leaders can bring back to senior leaders and confidently say it will contribute to the achievement of the goal, and ultimately the main objective. Your next generation leaders should develop as many strategies as possible with the resources – time, money, and especially people – available to the intervisions.

Another level of the plan is outlining the tactics to implement the strategies. This level is very detailed. For the previous strategy, tactics might include:

- Procuring a meeting room
- Posting respective leaders' availability
- Signing up for coaching and mentoring sessions (by employees)

If employees in this intervision are responsible for making sure they receive coaching and mentoring, then our main objective – through the cascading chain beginning with main objective to goal to strategy and now to tactic – has reached everyone in this intervision. You begin to see how everyone is touched by the main objective.

Concluding Thoughts

This chapter provides a picture of the contents of your strategy. The concept of a main objective has been discussed at length – the driving force of why you come into work every day. Beyond that, each intervision determines goals to satisfy the main objective. Next generation leaders and their people are included to implement very specific strategies and tactics. Chapter 3 begins with an example tying the idea of the main objective and goals together.

Chapter 2: Summary

■ Your main objective should drive your strategy and the strategic planning process. There are five characteristics for a main objective:

1. It should be grounded in the reality of your organization's present situation.
2. It should facilitate creative tension.
3. It should be the result of integrated thinking of the team, rather than a collection of individual objectives.
4. It should represent all key stakeholders – employees, customers, investors, etc.
5. It should invite and inspire people to want to bring it to fruition.

■ Be flexible as you continuously review your strategy as change always occurs.

■ Organizations that practice continuous review strategic planning make an average of 59 percent more strategic decisions annually than those focused on an annual review of an individual business unit.

■ The length of the strategic planning process may take 1 – 3 days to four months – based on the size of your organization.

■ Hold meetings off-site and use an external facilitator.

■ Strategic Planning generates creative tension.

- Organizational top leaders (president, CEO, etc.) should be patient during strategic planning and allow others to share their views first. This helps stimulate more discussion.

- The Strategy Chain is comprised of: main objective, goals, strategies and tactics.

- SMART = Specific, Measurable, Attainable, Relevant and Time-Based.

- What did you learn from the Strategy In Action?

Chapter 3

Chickens, Eggs & Strategy

"It's not a strategy when you only do things better.
It's a strategy when you do things different."
— Philip Kotler

If you have ever had the pleasure of attending a minor league baseball game, surely you have enjoyed the pure nature of the sport. Some of the best young baseball talent in the world, playing less for the money and more for the chance to one day make it to the Major Leagues, gives the minor-league game its character.

Suppose a minor league team sets its main objective to win as many games as possible in a season. If the players on the team are close to advancing to a big-league career; perhaps a good night at the plate or a solid pitching performance, does a conflict exist between the main objective of the team and the goals of the players?

Would it be better for a minor league team to recruit players who share the same objective of winning at the minor league level, regardless of advancement, to please the local fans? Or not bother with winning at all, and focus on individual goals – career advancement?

Is it more important to determine the needs of your people (players) or customers (fans) when creating your strategy? To properly answer this, let us take a closer look at both your people and customers. Perhaps a better understanding of how each group fits into strategy will help decide.

Of course, the people in your organization provide ideas for your strategy and perform the tactics in it. Surely then, it is necessary to have the right people in the right roles for the best performance. Getting the most out of your people is as important as getting the most out of your strategy. Chapter 6 considers this question by analyzing the AL^2A process of Ask, Listen, Learn and Act with people. Sections II and III discuss what comes first: the needs of the customers or employees (people) in determining how to create your strategy.

Chicken and Egg – People

Consider the old chicken and egg debate, "Which came first, the chicken or the egg?" In regard to strategy, which comes first, the strategy or the people who execute it? The answer to this question, though specific, is neither the "chicken or the egg," strategy or people. At no point in the strategic planning process is eliminating your top performers part of the process. You must create your strategy based on the main objective you previously created. People will need to be assigned specific roles for tasks to fulfill the main objective. Since people are the backbone of the strategy, they should help create it and execute it.

As the importance of a continuous review in strategy has been discussed, the AL^2A process is a continuous process as well. AL^2A is a process to Ask, Listen, Learn and Act on what your employees (people) do best and what they expect of your organization. Knowing

employees' knowledge, skills and abilities prior to planning is
important. However, with the continuous review process, learning
about your employees is continuous as well. So, the answer to which
comes first – people or strategy – presents a third option; your people
and your strategy interact in parallel. Determining employees' needs
and executing your strategy are both continuous review processes.

A similar question persists regarding customers' involvement in
your strategy. You would not be at the strategic level had you not
wisely attracted customers to your organization. Assuming you have
maintained a base of customers, do you create the strategy to suit
their needs? This would involve
the AL^2A process with
Customers. This proactively
answers why your customers do
business with you, what will

> Determining your employees'
> needs and executing your
> strategy are both continuous
> review processes.

encourage them to continue and how you'll act on this information.
Or, would you rather attempt to identify new customers that fit into
your strategy? Again, this question begins to look like the chicken
and egg scenario; which comes first, the strategy or the customers
that fit into it?

Chicken and Egg – Customers

The answer to this question is also not as simple as the chicken
or the egg. Both people and customers are certainly valuable to your
organization. Your customers have been providing you with revenue;
so their interests must be represented in your strategy. However,
going through this process might help you identify some unprofitable
customers. If the cost of keeping them as customers is not as much as
the revenue they create, we recommend firing customers – similar to

letting go an unproductive employee. As important as the customer piece is, the strategy must remain true to your main objective.

Even if customers do not fit your main objective exactly, similar to people, a customer's partnership can evolve. By assessing your present market situation, the AL^2A process to Ask, Listen, Learn and Act begins. This helps you gain an understanding of your customers' expectations of you. Should you want to maintain a healthy partnership with these customers, strategies need to be adapted during the life-cycle of the plan. Through a continuous review of your strategy, and continuous data gathering in the AL^2A process, the two interact in parallel.

As you can see, how you integrate people and customers with your strategy is really dependent on your present partnership with both groups – your present situation. A common process that should be avoided is saying, "Hey, we're just going to develop our strategy. We need help in many areas: We need to grow financially, we need to attract these customers, and we need to hire these employees. These are the key processes to focus on." This method of strategy creation lacks an analysis of the present situation.

This all too common process is done without data gathering. There are no intervision goals, no SMART strategies, no specific tactics, and no AL^2A with People or Customers – and certainly no main objective. At this level, there is no consideration for the present situation of the organization and how people and customers affect it. Sometimes, this is because a strategic planning process has not been developed throughout the organization. This course of action typically leads to three types of insufficient strategic plans:

1. Strategic Plans that exist only in the president's head. These may be well thought out, certainly well intended, but may not encompass the entire organization.

2. Strategic Plans not continuously reviewed. These may be well written and comprehensive; however, they are not given attention once the original process is completed.

3. Strategic Plans kept only to the leadership team and not communicated throughout the organization. These contradict the previous discussion on the importance of alignment. Alignment concerning both people and customers.

If any of these occur, they can be corrected. To correct type 1, in the president's head, the president must engage the organization to achieve buy-in from a great amount of individuals. In type 2, those not continuously reviewed, this can be corrected through a continuous review process. In type 3, plans kept only to the leadership team are fixed through a detailed communication process that cascades information throughout the organization.

Strategy In Action

Each of these strategic planning errors creates gaps in the message your strategy sends throughout the organization. A $50 million national construction company was struggling with these issues in their original strategic planning process. Issues such as these have many stakeholders – internal, external and contracting partners. Like other industries, their industry demands strategy to remain organized and competitive.

Upon reviewing their strategic planning process, the president mentioned a "continuous reviewed strategic plan" was in place. In later discussions with the president – who happens to have a finance background, formerly a CFO – we found the strategy to be financially focused. In fact, the financial portion (the goal pertaining to finances) was thoroughly documented and written. However, no other goals were specifically noted. This organization wanted to focus one goal on hiring, retaining and recruiting the right people for the next few years. The president pointed this out as important, yet there was no mention of it in the plan. This would correspond with the first problem mentioned, a strategic plan existing in the mind of the president.

The strategy also was not presented to anyone other than the leadership team, so the next generation leaders were not familiar with it. This organization had focused on integrating innovative ideas, and beginning lean production was one innovative focal point. Again, this item had been discussed in leadership team meetings, however, it was not documented anywhere – there were no SMART strategies pertaining to it. Lean production – a process of eliminating all types of waste in an organization's processes – is very quantifiable. Processes can be measured for improvement. Because of that, implementing strategies for lean fit well into the SMART rules previously discussed.

Unfortunately, in this instance, lean production was not communicated to anyone through the ranks. Like the third problem of strategic planning (Strategic Plans that are kept to the leadership team and not communicated throughout the organization), this example points out how a lack of employee engagement hinders communication of the strategy throughout the organization.

This organization deserves some credit as the previous strategy had been continuously reviewed. And, of course, they opted to work with an external facilitator on future strategic planning. Currently, items relating to people and lean production are represented, and their strategy has become more comprehensive.

Concluding Thoughts

Avoid strategic planning errors by asking questions about the strengths and weaknesses of your organization. Framed in a chicken or egg question, consider how both your people and customers affect strategy. A continuous review of the impact of both during the strategic planning process is recommended.

We have; however, avoided the question posed at the beginning of the chapter: Who is more important in strategic planning – people or customers?" Ideally, both people and customers need to be represented in your strategy. Determine your present situation, define how each is presently involved and then represent them accordingly in the strategy.

Chapter 3: Summary

■ People and Strategy interact in parallel version and both require a continuous review process.

■ How you integrate people and customers with your strategy is dependent on your presentation partnership with both groups.

■ There are three types of insufficient strategic plans:
1. Those existing only in the head of the president.
2. Those that are not continuously reviewed.
3. Those that are kept only to the leadership team and not communicated throughout the organization.

■ What did you learn from the Strategy In Action?

Chapter 4

Innovation

"The world leaders in innovation and creativity will also be world leaders in everything else."
– Harold R. McAlindon

Innovation is a hot topic, in the business world and on retailers' bookshelves. A recent web search turned up more books on innovation than on Leonardo Da Vinci.[1] However, we are concerned with innovation related to your strategy.[2] This chapter focuses on innovation as a component of your strategy and the processes involved with developing quality innovations.

Previous chapters have discussed the importance of strategy in keeping your organization aligned – on track – and ensuring your organization consistently performs its core competencies to a level that exceeds your customers' expectations. This is an adequate goal for an organization in its inception. Refining the things you do best is why you were able to create customers in the first place.

However, consider when the things you do best are not good enough anymore to retain those first customers, let alone find new ones. Your strategy, be it a financial goal, a human resource goal, or a market share goal, indicates growth. This is why innovation is a key piece of strategy. Innovation – the continuous development of products, services and/or processes – works in tandem with the development of your organization. As people in your organization develop products, services and/or processes, they utilize these to grow your organization.

People are imperative to innovation. As mentioned, as people innovate, they generate growth for their organization. In return, this growth provides them stability and incentives. This is a positive correlation between the incentive for people to innovate and innovation's positive effect on the organization.

What is important to consider and what is occasionally overlooked, is that all of an organization's people should be responsible for innovation. If all reap the benefits of innovation, then this is certainly true. Consider that innovation is not limited to developing new products and services, it also includes developing new processes. An improved process, possibly a lean production procedure to save time and money, has a positive impact on the bottom

> Innovation – the continuous development of products, services and/or processes – works in tandem with the development of your organization.

line and is every bit innovation. As your people improve at their jobs, it is their responsibility to innovate – to improve their processes – to maximize productivity and profitability.

Many companies designate certain individuals as innovators. "C-suite" managers who wear titles such as "Chief Marketing Officer," "Director, Design and Brand Experience," or the voguish new moniker "Chief Innovation Officer."[3] These individuals are perceived as having ambidextrous minds – comprehension in math and science, and sensibilities of the arts. They are designated as the drivers of their organizations' creativity – innovation.

As talented as they may be, are they the only people within the organization capable of innovation? Most likely not. Part of their duties are to foster an innovative environment for everyone. This is one key thing we would like to help you establish, that innovation is not the responsibility of any one person, or group of people – mainly senior leaders. Rather, it is the responsibility of senior leadership to make innovation a strategic goal, and communicate this goal – through the strategy – to all people within your organization.

Six Types of Innovations

There are six types of innovations that can flow throughout your organization. You can have more than one of the innovations. The key is to focus on aligning the innovation with your strategy.

The six types of innovations are:

1. **Big Bang Innovations** – These types of innovations seem to come out of nowhere. They are the most well known type of innovation because of the Big Bang's ability to rise quickly in popularity. These occur with the least frequency as inventors incubate for hours on their next big idea, which may or may not ever actually sell. Big Bangs are similar to fads – the next big thing that no one needs, yet many people purchase. A few dated examples include the Pet Rock or Hula Hoop. Big Bangs are becoming increasingly scarce as many ideas are already taken.

> It is the responsibility of senior leadership to make innovation a goal within your strategy.

2. **Quick Hitter Innovations** – These are innovations the market is ready and willing to purchase should they become available. Often, the innovator's first thought is, "Wouldn't it be great if I just had a (insert great idea here)." When

French Emperor Napoleon requested a new method for soldiers to read in the dark at night, Louis Braille developed the raised-dot reading system that shares his namesake. Though there was nothing like it preceding the innovation, there was already a demand for Braille.

3. **Always Broken Innovations** – These innovations are the opposite of the "if it isn't broken, don't fix it" mentality. Even if a product or service might be doing well, there is always room for improvement. Sometimes your customers' habits will let you know how to do it. A trip to any electronics retailer and a stroll past the MP3 player display (iPod comes to mind) is a lesson in the insatiable desire to accessorize. In Apple's mind, there is always room for improvement. Its incredibly popular product keeps getting smaller, remarkably, with a larger memory.

4. **Incognito Innovations** – These innovations sneak up on the marketplace. They are the byproduct of a previous, well performing product or service, with an unexpected twist. Consider the evolution of satellite radio. Traditional radio served as the general public's primary wireless communication means since the 1920's. Since then, traditional radio has been enjoyed by many, even as television and the Internet have gained prominence. Whether or not traditional radio needed improvement over this time span is debatable; however, few can argue that the general public was hoping for another radio option – especially from an extraterrestrial satellite. In 1992, commercial satellite radio was launched. At the time of this writing, XM and Sirius – the two U.S. owned companies – boast 10 million subscribers combined and are currently looking to merge

with each other to gain more efficiencies of scale. How
many saw this innovation coming?

5. **Survival Innovations** – These innovations are absolutely
necessary for the survival of a product or service. The
marketplace or other business environment forces decide if
the product or service becomes extinct if it does not undergo
some innovation. Consider the innovation of fuel injection in
automobile engines. Originally, the carburetor was the
device responsible for delivering fuel to an automobile
engine. It was not until the 1970's when government
regulation forced tighter restrictions on exhaust emissions
that the auto industry was forced to innovate. Fuel injection
delivers fuel more efficiently than the carburetor and is
acceptable by EPA imposed standards. The auto industry
was forced to innovate to keep cars on the road for the
survival of their product.[4]

6. **Sleeping Giant Innovations** – These are probably the most
difficult innovations to come by. The products or services
from which they stem are in decline, and the market is not
asking for anything new and/or improved. This puts the onus
on the innovators to innovate with only one piece of input
from the market: "What you have, we do not want." Would
anyone have predicted that Cadillac – one of General
Motors' struggling lines of automobiles – would have tried
to improve their brand by selling bicycles? In an attempt to
reach a younger, hipper buyer, Cadillac did just that.
Cadillac Accessories Manager Doug Schumacker thinks the
bicycles will have this effect, "The more unexpected brand
contacts we can have, the more surprising it is for the
consumer and the more chances we have to break through
preconceptions of what they think they know about Cadillac

now."[5] Notice this is not just innovative in the introduction
of the bicycle to the Cadillac product line; introducing a
bicycle to build brand equity is also an innovation in
Cadillac's marketing process.

As demonstrated in the prior six innovation paths, innovation is
not something confined to your organization. Actually, all innovation
comes from some customer input. With some innovations, it is the
organization's responsibility to observe its customers. Organizations
must gain a subliminal understanding of what customers want.

Whether these six innovation methods are agreeable or not, their
primary goal is the same: to understand the direction an organization
must take with innovation to completely satisfy customers. If
customers are not going to tell you how to innovate, you have to find
out somehow.

Strategy In Action

Fortunately for you, reading your customers for innovative cues
might not be as difficult as, well, spying. On occasion, your
customers will come right out and tell you what they want. A $3.5
billion global manufacturer in the food and beverage industry
experienced this as their largest customer told them exactly the
innovation they needed.

Having major retailers as top customers means focusing efforts
on supply chain management, particularly keeping the retailer's
shelves consistently stocked. In any perishable food industry,
effective supply chain management is a necessity. From the seeds
that grow the produce – be it for livestock feed or consumption – to
the food manufacturers, to the wholesalers or distribution centers,
and on to the neatly arranged shelves we see at our grocers, each step

in the chain must protect the viability of the fresh food. It is easy to take for granted an entire produce department full of fresh fruit and vegetables. That each item arrives unspoiled, despite long distances traveled, inclement weather and mishandling. The same is true for the meat department and frozen foods.

This particular customer places importance on consistently stocked shelves and will pay a premium for impeccable supply chain management. In the food business, space is a premium. Suppliers are awarded a certain amount of shelf space, and it is up to them to do their best with it – to maximize the space and fit the most product possible. The more that fits on the shelves, the more the customer can buy and reap a greater volume discount. Delivering unspoiled product efficiently adds much value to a supplier's product.

It stands to reason the customer would want the most efficient process possible. After all, what kind of retailer has empty shelves? It is frustrating, almost pointless, to shop where there is no guarantee that needed items will be in stock. The leading retailer is well aware of this and responds to the issue by maximizing shelf space and demanding its suppliers minimize container size.

One supplier, with a different product, yet the same packaging dilemma; was asked by the customer to innovate in order to improve supply chain efficiency. Innovation came in the form of an improved process, developing a space-efficient container to maximize shelf space. The source of innovation was straightforward – the customer indicated what they wanted. They tried numerous product packaging methods and eventually found one that maximized shelf space.

As an example (not a perishable example, though it will illustrate container size), consider the new refrigerator-friendly 12-pack soda containers. The old soda containers never really slid into a refrigerator in a way that made the cans accessible. The new ones allow for easy access and fit nicely in a small space.

We took a closer look at the two containers. The old style container has a volume of approximately 408 cubic inches. The new one has an approximate volume of 394 cubic inches. Not a tremendous difference at first glance; however, one soda can is approximately 24 cubic inches. The new container is more than half a can size smaller. To the consumer, this appears to be an innovation designed to help them fit soda in their fridge. Regardless, we would be curious to ask the soda manufacturers where the inspiration for innovation came – market demand or supply-chain efficiency? Whichever the source, the innovation has become an advantage to meet demand for consumers and improve supply-chain efficiency.

In this situation, the food manufacturer would have benefited by implementing an AL^2A process. This process proactively identifies customers' needs, including opportunities for innovation. The choice becomes yours, to wait for your customers to come and tell you how to innovate, or to go ask them.

The Road to Growth is Paved with Good Innovations

Innovations are derived through one of six paths. Looking back at the six types of innovations, note that each is essentially a different method by which innovation occurs. Innovation is not limited to Big Bangs, the ideas that appear to pop out of thin air. They miraculously meet some market niche without a predecessor product that either flourished or failed. Because these are some of the most memorable innovations, there is a common perception that Big Bangs are innovation and every other product development is something else. Rather, innovations develop through a process with regularly occurring simultaneous steps. Of the six processes, Big Bangs have the fewest steps and are viewed as a shortcut to success. Stay away from get-rich-quick ideas and focus on a process for actual innovation.

All innovations are one of two things:
- Brand new ideas unrelated to your existing products or services.
- Ideas that have characteristics similar to your existing products or services, yet other characteristics that differentiate them.

Consider the first category, Brand New Ideas. If there is no market for a brand new idea – no matter how clever it is – there is no point in developing it for sale. Determining the way the market asks for the product or service is what divides the brand new idea into two distinct innovation types. Each brand new idea is requested by the market in one of two ways:

o <u>Proactively</u>. Customers express what they want through a statement or testable quantitative analysis. These customers will actively show you they know what they want.
o <u>Subliminally</u>. Innovators observe customers to determine what they want or do not want through monitoring purchasing habits. These customers will subliminally show you they know what they want.

Along with brand new ideas, it was also mentioned ideas can have characteristics similar to your existing products or services. This sort of innovation comes from either of the following:

▪ <u>Enhancements of existing products that are established and are doing well</u>. This is where a lot of products come from, yet are not typically considered innovation. However, the development of these products or services, or the

enhancement of the product or service line, can benefit sales
every bit as much and more than a new innovation. Think
accessories or products stating they are "new and improved."

- Enhancements on existing products and services that are not
doing well. Rather than abandoning these ideas, innovation
is finding the best part of what is left and evolving that into
something positive.

These innovations – those similar to existing products and
services – are also subject to the demand of customers. The market
will either proactively or subliminally communicate their level of
demand. Graphic 4.1 aids in this understanding:

Graphic 4.1: Paths to Innovation

Innovation Paths

Brand New ideas

New Ideas Similar to Old Ideas

Active
Quick Hitters

Passive
Big Bangs

Products Doing Well

Products Not Doing Well

Active
Always Broken

Passive
Incognito Innovations

Active
Survival Innovations

Passive
Sleeping Giants

Each innovation follows a distinct path. Each begins either as a brand new idea (one no one has ever thought of before – these are rare), or an idea that is a twist on an old idea (more common). Beyond that, the brand new ideas are either items the market is actively clamoring for (Braille) or something passive (those that sneak up on consumers, like the dated Pet Rock).

On the other side, there are products that are doing well and those that are not. Of the products that are doing well, some always seem to need improvement (iPod with its perpetual accessories and updated editions) and those that sneak up a bit (satellite radio). Of the products not doing well, there are those that the market is actively asking for (fuel injection) and those they are never expecting (the Cadillac bicycle).

Innovation as a Process

As you can see, there are a variety of ways your organization can arrive at innovation. It is important to understand that innovation is a process. Part of the process is the facilitation of ideas from your people. To do this, it is senior leadership's responsibility to get everyone thinking – to create a culture of innovation. This is the broad goal, and within it there are strategies and tactics to develop innovative thinking.

One tactic is an innovation session (see Graphic 4.2), an intensive event designed to bring together your sharpest minds for the purpose of sharing ideas. Include 10 – 20 people, including some suppliers and customers as it is encouraged to get fresh perspectives involved in this type of process. Sometimes, innovation is stunted because the people closest to certain products, services and processes have been close for so long; it is difficult for them to look at the familiar from a different perspective. Include those who are highly creative, new hires and/or recent graduates.

Graphic 4.2: Innovation Session

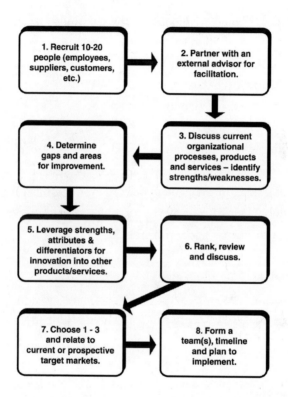

A facilitator can be helpful in getting everyone involved. Unfortunately, office status quo may inhibit free dialogue. This is especially so when it comes to admitting something that has always been done one way may need improvement. An experienced facilitator serves as a creative catalyst to get people talking and buffer against criticism.

At a recent conference, a facilitator briefly demonstrated an outsider's ability to trigger innovation in another firm. The presenter

asked someone in the audience to volunteer what their organization
manufactured or specialized in. An individual obliged, mentioning
his organization manufactured high-end airline seats. It took no more
than a few minutes of brainstorming for the audience to come back
with several innovations including diversifying into horizontal
markets such as the auto industry, or other similar structured seating
markets. This innovation seems obvious now that it had been said,
yet at the time, the volunteer
had not thought of it.
Sometimes, it takes someone
objective and unbiased to open
the door for innovation.

> An innovation session is an
> intensive event designed to bring
> together your sharpest minds for
> the purpose of sharing ideas.

Approximately 2-5 percent of ideas at the session should become
hot topics. These are areas that your organization must innovate
immediately to either improve a struggling product, service or
process, or to stay on pace with an industry standard.

Innovation and Your Strategy

Innovation as it is being presented here is ultimately a function
of your overall strategy. For organizational growth, innovation must
be considered as a goal of your strategy.

Through Section I, the components of a strategic plan have been
segmented into four steps:
1. Main Objective
2. Goals
3. Strategies
4. Tactics

Include innovation as one of the goals. This allows everyone in your company to recognize innovation as the invisible hand moving your organization towards improvement and growth.

Reasoning for the importance and sequence of each step in the strategy has been given, as well as the importance of continuously reviewing the entire plan. Now that you have an understanding of the depth of a strategy, Sections II and III delve into the importance of the two most important stakeholders in an organization – people and customers.

Section II provides further detail of exactly how to integrate people into your strategy. The AL^2A process will be discussed in more specific terms throughout this section to help you identify how your best people can positively impact your organization.

Beyond that, Section III specifies precisely how to involve your customers into your strategy. The AL^2A process receives a more detailed analysis to ensure your strategy helps attract and retain the best customers for the longevity of your organization.

The partnership of your organization with its people and its customers is the next most important item to ensure your strategy is not a mistake. A recent conference presenter pointed out the difference between two commonly used terms – *failures* and *mistakes*. A failure was defined as "a learning experience… something negative occurs, but the individual learns from the experience and it doesn't happen again." A mistake, on the other hand, was defined as "an experience that does not have learning… an individual has a negative experience, but does not learn from it, and it may occur again."[6]

The presenter was not speaking specifically about people or customers, or strategy for that matter; regardless, the more we reflected, strategy lends a hand in avoiding mistakes. Strategy affords you the ability to learn from your *failures,* and not consistently make *mistakes.*

Concluding Thoughts

Strategy is one component of our puzzle. Throughout your organizational journey your strategic decisions will impact which piece of the puzzle you begin with. Unfortunately, in the entire lifetime of your organization, some decisions will be failures. With all the variables in your environment, it is impossible to predict what will happen in every situation, as inevitably, a wrong decision is made. You, however, have a strategy. You can learn from the failure – the wrong turn – and get back on track. The wisdom learned from that failure will help you make a better decision the next time you are deciding which puzzle piece to use. Just remember to look at the puzzle as a complete entity, so all pieces fit perfectly together.

Chapter 4: Summary

■ Innovation is the continuous development of products, services and/or processes. It works in tandem with the development of your organization.

■ Everyone should be responsible for innovation.

■ Innovation should be a goal within your strategy.

■ There are six types of innovation:
   1. Big Bang
   2. Quick Hitter
   3. Always Broken
   4. Incognito
   5. Survival
   6. Sleeping Giant

■ All innovations are one of two things:
   • Brand new ideas, not related to your existing products or services.
   • Ideas that have characteristics similar to your existing products or services, yet other characteristics that differentiate them.

■ Hold an Innovation Session. This is an event designed to bring together your sharpest minds to share ideas and innovate.

■ What did you learn from the Strategy In Action?

Section II

People

"Whatever your life's work is, do it well.
A man should do his job so well that the living,
the dead and the unborn could do it no better."
– Martin Luther King, Jr.

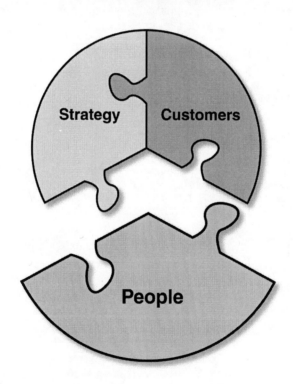

As previously mentioned, People is the term we are using to define your employees, associates, partners, team members, workers, labor or human capital. The following three chapters outline the steps to maximizing the potential of people in your organization.

Like any resource, there must be planning to gain the maximum utility from it. Though people are a resource, they are unique in their ability to think, act and feel on their own intuition. This is what makes working with people one of the most interesting aspects of leading a business, not to mention the most challenging. This challenge begins with determining the roles within your organization that are needed – and the skill levels required by people to perform in these roles. Beyond that, finding the people with whom you are most comfortable entrusting your organization and ensuring that you retain them for as long as possible are consistent challenges.

Communication is an essential tool to solve the retention problem. This is not limited to just being heard by your people. Rather, effective communication refers to clear, consistent and usually concise messages about your organization. Poor communication from superiors to their direct reports is the number one reason people leave an organization. Overcoming this is not as difficult as many have been led to believe.[1]

This book began with a discussion of strategy, and no strategic initiative is complete without input and feedback from your people. The AL^2A (Ask, Listen, Learn, Act) process provides your organization with an opportunity to assess people's (employees') current reality, and align their goals with those of the organization. Chapter 6 demonstrates how AL^2A provides the bookends related to People and Customers surrounding your Strategy. As discussed in Section I, this alignment between people, their intervisions, and corporate strategy is imperative to fulfill long-term goals and your main objective.

Chapter 5

Roles, Positions and People

*"I tell you and you forget. I show you
and you remember. I involve you and you understand."*
– Eric Butterworth

We begin this chapter discussing the strategy for your people. Why are people a main component of your strategy? In our initial discussion of strategy, we mentioned two areas – people and customers – that need special consideration. This chapter begins to look at the importance of your people. Why should you have a people plan? And why do certain roles have a more strategic impact than others?

Chapter 1 discussed why a strategy is needed. The strategic plan is divided into the main objective, goals, strategies and tactics. The people portion of your strategy is important for several reasons. First, people should be reflected in at least one of your goals (i.e., how to attract and develop the right people to benefit your organization). Second, people in your organization will execute the strategy. Without finding and developing the right people, and then relying on them to implement the strategies and tactics in the plan, the entire process is futile.

The 4 R's

Inevitable with growth, you may need to add new people, though that is not always the case. Often, we see organizations whose entire solution for growing pains is to add more people. There is a time and place to add people – doing so should not be the first option. Retaining employees is as important as recruiting new ones. After all, the people already in your organization know their jobs and the goals. Losing people because of growth causes a twofold problem – you do not have anyone to perform the current work and you still must find others. A basic, sensible approach to finding and keeping the right people in your organization is the 4 R's. This represents:

- Recruiting
- Retraining
- Rewarding
- Retention

Recruiting people is important. It is the initial step in the process and can become expensive if the right people are not recruited. Your Human Resources area should focus on alignment with the corporate culture in determining a good fit. In many areas, skills can be learned; however, cultural fit is more difficult. Human Resources should seek prospective people that are able to identify with your organization to become fully engaged.

With growth, and the implementation of certain strategic items and tactics, people will encounter new tasks. **Retraining** your people on their new functions is important. You need to provide people with the time, resources and tools to perform their jobs. Ongoing training is critical. Workshops, mentor programs, memberships and technology are some ways this can be accomplished. People cannot be expected to become engaged in their new tasks if there is no training. As much hope or confidence you have in their abilities to learn without help, the reality is some retraining is necessary to get the job done right.

Rewarding is another step to engage people. Money isn't always the key reward. Rewarding is a major step for people to truly identify with your organization. Providing opportunities for advancement and the right work/life balance opportunities will help transform regular people into engaged people.

The fourth R is **retention** – keeping your people. If people are engaged, they will stay

> The 4 R's of People:
> Recruiting, Retraining,
> Rewarding and Retention

longer. They will even recruit others, spread the good word and become employee evangelists. They are the people that will help valuable and loyal customers.

Each of these R's relates to engaging people. Remember, engaged people are those who do meaningful work that they *and* the organization value. These people enjoy their jobs so much they are even willing to work for a lower salary than the industry average for their position.

In today's virtual world and changing business climate, it is easier for people to jump ship than ever before. The Internet provides broad networking opportunities for people and allows for almost limitless job searches. After investing the time and money to recruit and train people, it is necessary to take measures to retain them. It has been calculated, on the low end, that the cost of one employee turning over is 150 percent of their annual wage.[1] That is a cost of $75,000 for an employee paid $50,000 annually. Assuming this is average compensation for all people, 10 percent turnover for an organization of 100 amounts to expenses of $750,000; and for a mid-sized company of 1,000, 10 percent turnover equates to an expense of $7.5 million.

If the sheer costs of turnover are not incentive enough to retain people, the long term health and vitality of your organization should be. As current senior leaders grow in their careers, they also grow in age. Planning for succession is an honest consideration, especially as today's baby boomer generation continues to plan for retirement. At the time of this writing, there were nearly 83 million baby boomers (Americans born between 1946 and 1964) alive in America. Most of them will retire by 2010, leaving a shortage of workers, many which are senior leaders. It would be comforting to know the organization you worked so hard to grow is in the hands of someone who has been around for a while.

The current reality of workplace turnover is there are no guarantees. To protect against the seizure of your organization's productivity by turnover, building bench strength to step in when needed is a critical element of your people plan.

People In Action

A global $1 billion provider of identification solutions innovated a way of ensuring it retains the best bench strength for future growth.

With nearly 6,000 people globally, identifying top performers is strategically important for them. Senior leaders from the leadership team invest up to four hours per month going through a process to select who are their best of the best. This list is only one percent of the entire organization, equating to approximately 60 people. For another four hours per month, the leadership team holds a separate meeting discussing these 60 people; identifying their skill gaps, their available opportunities, and their development plan – basically their long-term growth potential.

This strategy ensures the right people are ready when there is turnover in key positions. These people are not only promoted based

on turnover, as the organization needs key people in strategic or
leadership roles, these people are able to step into these roles. This
organization is also active in mergers and acquisitions, averaging
seven to 10 annually. The best-of-the-best group becomes prospects
for acquisition integration leadership roles, and another realm of
training and development begins when this occurs. If the person does
well as acquisition integration leader, they ultimately can be selected
to lead the newly acquired business.

You can begin to see why a people plan is so important in
conjunction with your strategy. Having engaged people doing the
work – 'A' people as we refer to them – can be a major benefit to
your organization (a definition of A people is provided later in this
chapter). People willing to do more for less are bound to be top
performers if they are matched with the right role for their skill set.
All your people should be comfortable with and engaged in what
they are doing, and it will be easier to attract and retain. It is
becoming extremely difficult to replace the highest performing
people if they leave for other opportunities. However, many
companies are only concerned with branding their products and
services, and they forget the need to brand themselves to prospects.
Think of recruits as potential customers and use marketing analysis
to identify competition and attributes that matter most to recruits and
how to attract them – strategize to attract and retain people.

Potential

It has been said that people possess five core strengths, along
with several developmental opportunities (weaknesses). Within each
of these – weak and strong – people's strengths rarely change.[2] They
are elements of an ingrained personality; at least, and not subject to
change through any immediate practice. Based on our experiences

and research, people can improve their weaknesses with practice, although they rarely displace one of their top five core strengths.

If you will imagine, each of your people is bound, to a degree, to some inherent personality characteristics. Assume a top and bottom five exists infinitely. Then, how do people improve? In the context of the workplace, these traits manifest themselves as varying degrees of performance in different areas. This is why quality management of people is so important. Strengths must be cultivated, weaknesses developed, and all of the traits in between – the many other characteristics a person is not defined by – must be strengthened, in an effort to maximize a person's potential.

> Strengths must be cultivated, weaknesses developed, and all other traits must be strengthened to fully maximize potential.

People In Action

In Section I, we discussed a $3.5 billion global manufacturer in the food and beverage industry. This organization has a strategy to accentuate the positive in each of its potential senior leaders. It is also focused on ensuring that each of its people understands the functions of its Operations area. The nature of its business is manufacturing, so Operations is the pulse of the organization, and they feel everyone, specifically those aspiring to be leaders, must have competency in it.

As in any organization, there are varying skill sets within intervisions. Human Resources people, Marketing people and Finance people all bring diverse skill sets; and as individuals, they exhibit their own strengths and weaknesses. This organization feels if the skills necessary to master Operations are not inherent in each next generation leader, then the skills must be learned.

Each next generation leader is required to work in an Operations position for up to two years. The organization feels so strongly about this, it is a requirement for advancement. In our experiences, some time may be necessary; however, top performers – the organization's next leaders –should help decide the length of their time based on their individual performance. If a person is truly dedicated to learning the processes of Operations, six months may be adequate.

This strategy of cross-functional involvement allows each of these people the opportunity to either enhance a strength or recognize a developmental area. Because they return to an advanced position after successfully completing time in Operations, recognizing the developmental area is crucial to career growth. This experience allows these people to broaden their skill set, providing them some Operations knowledge, and leverage that with their core skills (i.e., Human Resources, Marketing Finance, etc.). Essentially, this strategy provides both the organization and the people an opportunity to realize their potential – not necessarily as Operations people, rather people with specific strengths and weaknesses.

The New First 'R'

Your people plan is a comprehensive view of the human capital – people – that make up your organization. These people become embedded somewhere in your organization. Somewhere means they are strategically placed in a strategically designed role. It was mentioned that people ultimately will implement your strategy. For example, you cannot have an organization of all leaders. This allows for plenty of people to plan the strategy, and none to do the actual execution – the work. Fortunately for you and many others, as labor becomes more and more specialized, it is evident that different people are more effective at different tasks. Some are better at strategy, some at planning and some at executing.

Your people plan now begins to take shape as a two part process. Performing the four R's – recruiting, retraining, rewarding and retaining – is vital. However, the fifth R – **Roles** – really becomes the first R as we analyze the sequence a bit closer. Organizations can bring in the most talented people in the world in their respective positions; however, if they are assigned the wrong

> Roles – the fifth R – is really the first R as it must be completed before anything else.

roles, is there any chance for their success? The odds are better if people and roles are matched perfectly.

It is difficult to say the Green Bay Packers would have fared as well in their 1996 NFL Super Bowl championship had the late star defensive-end Reggie White been brought in to play the quarterback role, and 3-time NFL MVP quarterback Brett Favre had been assigned a defensive-end role. White may have been able to throw a football, but not with the distance and accuracy of Favre. Favre on the other hand, is noted to be one of the toughest players in NFL history, yet is a bit undersized for a defensive end.

Like professional football players, most people in your organization are probably talented in other ways as well. There is a method to determine the strategic importance of your organization's roles while insuring people are capable of handling this importance are inserted into these roles. The method insures people are placed in roles that reflect the role's strategic importance.

Classifying Roles and People

The following information may appear to take a long time to accomplish – and it may. Yet, it is vital to achieve a successful

people strategy. Once completed, the process becomes much easier
when done thereafter.

Four distinct values for each role in an organization have been
identified. Roles A through D have been ranked based on their
importance related to strategy and the level to which the performance
of the role varies. Not to be confused with pay or hierarchy, these
roles score favorably if they are
deemed imperative to the
execution of strategy. Beyond
that, people need to be ranked
in their abilities and fit with the
organization. Then, the two will
be matched – roles and people –
resulting in high performers in
strategic roles, not the poor performers.

> We have identified four distinct values for each role in any organization. Roles A through D are graded based on their importance related to strategy and the level to which the performance of the role varies.

The Classification of roles:

A. **'A' roles have the greatest impact on the organization's
    strategy.** They are also the rarest roles in the workforce – no
    more than 20 percent.[3] These roles are unique in that
    variation in the quality of the job performance is very high;
    meaning one individual can perform this job very well,
    another very poorly. (Compare the skilled heart surgeon to a
    resident physician.) The more of these highly variable roles
    an organization has, the more competitively it differentiates
    itself.

    However, a role does not have to be highly variable or
    difficult to be strategic. A bank we are familiar with employs
    a person at the entrance that greets every person by name,
    along with a smile and "hello". This helps execute their
    strategic element of providing friendly service.

B. **'B' roles offer support for the strategic roles.** However, they do not offer the performance variability of A roles, so B's provide less of a competitive advantage. B roles do not really create value as much as they maintain it. Roles such as department supervisors or project managers may fall into this category.

C. **'C' roles have little effect on strategy.** There is not much variability in the performance of different people in these roles. That is not to say there are not good workers in these roles. There may be, for instance, a standardized process that inhibits anyone from excelling in this type of role. This is typical in a production line role. For example, in the Toyota production system, there are processes to standardize the sequence of operations in a single process which leads a floor worker to produce quality goods efficiently (and consistently).[4] Because of these standards, technically, you or I should be able to step onto a Toyota production line and work efficiently. These roles, characteristic of substitutability, contribute to its downgrading.

D. **'D' roles have no impact on strategy.** Anyone can do these jobs because there is nothing important to do. There is no value added to customers or the organization in these roles. These roles should be eliminated immediately.

A precise way to calculate the ranking of roles is to assign a value to both the effect on performance variability and strategic effect. Each variable is measured on a scale of 1 to 10 (see Graphic 5.1). Scores are graphed on an 'X' and 'Y' axis, with the roles ranking high in both categories – A roles – in quadrant one. Quadrant two is B roles because they are higher on strategy, yet low in variability. Quadrant three is C roles, as they are lower on strategic effect, yet have higher performance variability. And quadrant four is D roles, low in both, and should be eliminated.

Graphic 5.1: Role Rating

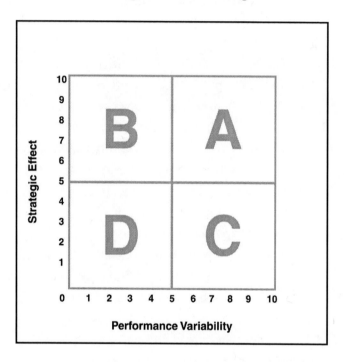

We suggest using a similar process to evaluate people (see Graphic 5.2). People are rated on a 1 to 10 scale using different variables than the role analysis. For this, use a culture scale and a performance scale. The culture scale measures a person's fit with the organization's culture. The performance piece is the person's ability to do their job correctly using the same scale. Use the four letter system A – D for people so they can be applied to the system for roles. Thereby aligning A – D roles with A – D people.

   A. 'A' people are the highest performing and most culturally fit people in your organization. If they are not currently your senior leaders, they should be next generation leaders. In most cases, A people belong in A roles. There may be some instances where an A person does not yet fit in an A role. Not all A roles are leadership roles. Somewhere in your organization there will be an important role for these people, in some cases it may be a B role. Typically though, A people deserve A roles.

B. 'B' people rate high on the culture scale, yet may slightly lag in performance. This may not be their fault. It may be they are still learning their job or have not received proper training. Regardless, they are committed to the culture of the organization –not always easy to find. The good thing about B people is they can be trained, possibly even to be A people. Their commitment to the organization must be rewarded, and typically B people are placed in B roles.

C. 'C' people rate high on the performance scale and lower on the culture scale. For now, these people usually will have a hard time finding their way out of C roles. Consider the trainability of the B person. Though lower in performance, their positive cultural fit indicates they are willing to learn and may improve performance. Improving cultural fit – attitude in a sense – is more difficult to train. C people may perform well today; however, the reality is their lack of cultural fit will most likely contribute to their exit from the organization. Finding B people with the cultural fit and the ability to improve their performance is a better option when promoting. C people should be informed of their situation and a performance improvement plan should be created for them. Improvement should be shown in 30 – 60 days or they should be removed from your organization.

D. 'D' people are both low in performance and cultural fit.
These people do not "get it" and probably do not care, as is
indicated by their low performance. They should be
eliminated immediately. If already in D positions, consider
eliminating the position altogether. If D people are in A to C
roles, they should be removed from your organization.

Graphic 5.2: People & Culture Rating

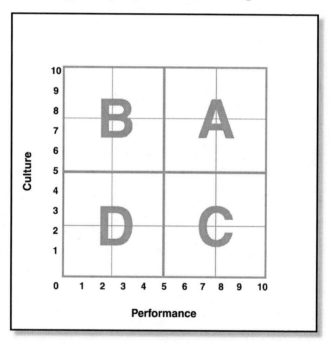

If your organization is large enough – like the one in our first
example of this chapter with 6,000 employees – each individual
people quadrant can be subdivided into another four sections (see
Graphic 5.2). For instance, the 'A' section might be 1,500 people if
using the previous example, so it is necessary to subdivide and
subdivide to analyze who the best of the best performers are, who

needs training, which fit the culture and so on. This is how the firm arrives at its top performer list of 60 people out of 6,000.

Continuing to Continuously Review

This entire people process is a key part of strategy. It must be implemented and reviewed on a timeline with the strategic planning process. We have discussed reviewing the strategy on at least a quarterly basis, and depending on the size of your organization, as often as weekly (for larger organizations). The fit between people and strategy is so important that this people plan deserves the same attention. After all, people execute the strategy – having A people to execute it is vital for success.

While there are many systems and trainings to engage your people, we have created a process called AL^2A (Ask, Listen, Learn & Act) that we believe is the most effective.

Chapter 5: Summary

■ The 4 R's are: recruiting, retraining, rewarding and retention.

■ People typically have five core strengths. These strengths must be cultivated, weaknesses developed, and all other traits must be strengthened to fully maximize potential.

■ Roles – the fifth R – is actually the first R as it must be completed before anything else.

■ 'A' roles have the greatest impact on organizational strategy. 'A' people should be in these roles.

■ What did you learn from the People In Action?

Chapter 6

Ask, Listen, Learn & Act (AL²A)

"Desire is the key to motivation, but it's the determination and commitment to an unrelenting pursuit of your goal – a commitment to excellence – that will enable you to attain the success you seek."
– Mario Andretti

Goals are carefully crafted, measurable items which set your organization's standard for success. They must be realistically attainable and grounded in a current realistic situation.

AL²A (Ask, Listen, Learn & Act) provides organizations with an opportunity to assess your people's (employees') current reality. The present situation is contrasted with a desired situation, and attainable goals are set to reach the desired situation.

The Bookends of Strategy

AL²A is a newly created process providing the bookends related to People and Customers that surround your overall Strategy (see Graphic 6.1). It consists of four steps: [1]

1. **Ask:** interact with your people by proactively asking about their needs.
2. **Listen:** understand what they are asking for and/or needing.
3. **Learn:** take this feedback seriously and identify why gaps may exist.
4. **Act:** create an action plan and close any identified gaps.

Graphic 6.1: AL^{2}A as the Bookends of Strategy

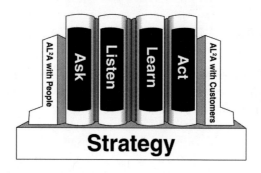

Your organization may already offer an employee satisfaction survey; however, very few organizations offer AL^{2}A.

Beginning with an assessment of your people's perceptions and ending with the same from your customers, AL^{2}A provides you with the before and after of strategy. Imagine for example, if you had never considered how to form your strategy. As more minds think better than few, you would certainly want to ask some people, possibly those within and outside your organization.

This – Ask, Listen, Learn and Act from everyone in your organization – is an intensive process. Like anything new, it may initially take some time to get the process going; however, once people learn it and become emotionally engaged with it, the time is reduced – especially in relation to the return on investment. It also seems inefficient to ask people one question at a time, and if you have already begun a process, consider asking several questions relating to many categories. Before you know it, the AL^2A process has begun.

(I Don't Need No) Satisfaction

> The number of "engaged people"– rather than satisfied people – you have is a better determinant to the success of an organization. On average, only 29% of people are fully engaged at work.

A key to the AL^2A process is not only to focus on people satisfaction. If satisfaction is all you are looking for from your people, you are aiming too low. Satisfied people are usually content with their work situation. Getting these people to show-up and contribute is not a problem, and chances are, compensation is adequate. So, momentarily, the relationship is probably fair for both parties. Unfortunately, terms such as *show-up*, *adequate* and *fair* lend more to complacency than satisfaction. Not all satisfied people are complacent people, yet there are similarities.

Now, the number of engaged people you have – rather than satisfied people – is a better determinant to the success of an organization. On average, only 29% of employees are fully engaged at work.[2] Engaged people have excellent attendance and safety records, outperform others in productivity and profitability, have higher retention rates, and offer greater customer satisfaction. In contrast, more than 50% of employees arrive at work and perform the bare minimum – just enough to sustain employment. These disengaged employees cost companies about $300 billion a year in lost profits and damaged customer relationships.[3] These statistics demonstrate that effectively managing and measuring employee engagement can add value to your bottom line.

Compare a satisfied customer to a _completely_ satisfied customer. A satisfied customer has done business with you in the past and will continue to until a lower price or better incentive from a competitor comes along. These customers are not *completely satisfied.* If they were, they would know how good the relationship they have is, and give you an opportunity to retain it.

Compare this satisfied customer to a satisfied employee. While these people have been around for a while; if another position comes along, would they take the position without giving you a chance to retain them? This moves the term satisfied people to engaged people to "emotionally engaged people."[4] People whose ties to the organization extend beyond compensation and benefits; those with an emotional attachment, a lifestyle, and comfort level with the organization and a belief their work contributes to the achievement of something they believe in.

Chris Berman, world-renowned sportscaster for ESPN, is an example of an emotionally engaged employee. It is reported that in 1989, NBC offered him $800,000 to leave ESPN. At the time, he was making $185,000. He asked ESPN if his salary could come close to this offer. ESPN offered $600,000 and he stayed.[5] His willingness to stay for a 25 percent lower salary says a great deal about his emotional attachment – not to mention his trust to approach leadership and discuss this with them – without asking to match or beat the NBC salary. This also demonstrates a great relationship between Berman and leadership as he was proactive in approaching leadership to have an open and honest discussion about this.

Satisfied customers are to satisfied people as completely satisfied customers are to emotionally engaged people. The latter groups, completely satisfied customers and emotionally engaged people, are those that stay through the tough times. This is why people are being discussed before customers, because emotionally engaged people are more productive and result in providing customers with better service. This creates long-lasting, completely satisfied customers.

Ask

In a time when recruiting and retaining people can be a differentiator, organizations need to understand why people choose to remain (or leave). The first step of AL^2A is to ask your people by gathering their voice. Ask includes up to three-phases.

1. Employee Satisfaction Questionnaire. This asks questions to determine if people are dissatisfied, complacent or completely satisfied. This also provides your organization with intervision information related to corporate culture, career development and working conditions.

2. Employee Engagement Analysis. This is a validated, standardized tool to measure engagement. Years ago, The Gallup Organization created 12 specific questions related to employee engagement.[6] The analysis hones in on how well people feel their efforts are aligned with

> To identify your distinct functional areas, we have created a new term – intervisions – or "visions together." Your intervisions work cohesively sharing the same vision; with the strategy as the means to the objective as the end.

strategy, if they are empowered, if their efforts promote collaboration across the organization, and if they are supported in their personal continuous development.

3. 360-Degree Review. This allows people to rate themselves, while also receiving feedback from their leader, peers and direct reports (if they have them). It also provides people with personalized training opportunities to develop skills in areas such as teamwork, leadership, communications and others.

Many organizations already complete one – or even two – of these (i.e., employee satisfaction, employee engagement, or the 360-degree analysis). We have found very few organizations that have a process for implementing all three across the organization in one combined process. The process is based on four assumptions our research has proven to be necessary to achieve ultimate success. These include the 4 C's:

> We have found very few organizations that have a process for implementing all three phases across the organization in one combined process.

- Confidentiality. Employee information filtered directly to HR may not be as valid as if going to an independent third party. Many people feel that HR and leadership will know how they respond to questions and they will "get in trouble." At a minimum, have a third party receive and filter the information as this will alleviate any concerns and provide for the best information.[7]

- Communication. This will be discussed in more detail in Chapter 7, and for purposes related to AL^2A, prior to beginning this process, communication must occur. The process should be communicated 2 to 3 times to all people via the best communication vehicles for your organization.[8]

- Concise. AL^2A must ask enough questions to gather detailed information, yet not be too long that your people avoid investing the time to take it, or be afraid to take it.[9]

- Customized. While many categories and questions are consistently based on best practices and experience, up to 50 percent can be different. As every organization and its people are different, AL^2A is not intended to provide exactly the same categories and questions time and time again.

The 4 C's are always part of the process – in addition to combining employee satisfaction, employee engagement and a 360-degree review. The first step of Ask digs deeper into asking about specific items related to your people and organization – customization for each organization. For example, an Employee Satisfaction Questionnaire may include specific categories about:

- Culture
- Leadership
- Teamwork
- Satisfaction
- Communication

> Categories and questions must be customized and personalized for each and every organization as every organization – and its people – are different.

The culture of each organization is different, as is its leadership philosophies, teamwork, structure, etc. The process is designed to vary from organization to organization. One organization requested a specific category and questions related to Lean Operations as they were just implementing this and wanted a baseline measure. Another organization was very focused on community involvement and requested a specific category and questions about this.

As this is employee satisfaction, you may not see a category of Engagement in your own survey if you currently offer one. While some organizations may ask engagement questions using a completely separate system, AL^{2}A incorporates this.

AL^{2}A has an engagement category that closely follows Gallup's 12 questions.[10] Taken with the other components of AL^{2}A and using a slight re-wording of the Net Promoter Score question,[11] we pose, "I would recommend Company X as a place to work to a friend or colleague." Other questions in each category vary greatly from organization to organization.[12]

Before moving to Listen and Learn, two other items related to Ask must be addressed. First, 360-reviews are offered by many organizations.[13] While a great tool, this is not something to offer all people at once as it can be a lengthy and time consuming process – especially for leaders with multiple direct reports as they will have to complete these for each direct report. AL^2A has the ability to offer 360-reviews as part of one overall people process, aligned with emotional engagement (satisfaction and engagement), to as many people as your organization chooses. Combining anything into one process always has benefits compared to separate systems and databases of information. This part of the Ask element is largely effective when linked to Performance Management.[14]

Questions can be placed on a 1-7 or 1-10 scale, ranging from Completely Disagree (1) to Completely Agree (7 or 10, depending upon the scale).

Listen and Learn

As people are providing quantitative and qualitative feedback, another venue of qualitative information gathering is to "walk the floor." Leaders should take time every week to walk around the offices, cubicles, operations lines, etc. listening where their people are working. By doing so, they can observe what is occurring, how morale is, how people are acting, etc. It also allows people to ask questions and gain information. Senior leaders should do this across all interversions and locations, and leaders with teams at multiple locations should schedule monthly or quarterly visits to walk the floor and engage people.

Once information is gathered, it must be analyzed, as you should have information to Learn from and include as part of your strategy. Granted, not all people are affected by everything that happens at a high strategic level. Line-level people and some next generation leaders – though impacted indirectly – may not be involved on a day-to-day basis with some items such as acquisition strategy for the next year. Regardless, you have now captured information on the general consensus of what your people expect from the organization in the future. As people are undeniably important in the direction of your organization, with newfound knowledge, you yield innovative solutions to further improve collaborative efforts with them. These solutions continuously enhance organizational effectiveness.

Not only is AL^2A a useful process to measure people's needs collaboratively and individually, the information can be categorized by intervision.[15] For instance, if an analysis of the entire organization was completed, and further analysis was needed in your marketing area (possibly because of some identified gaps); the data could be analyzed to represent the voice of marketing people collectively.

Similarly, if a particular location required further analysis, the information could be divided to represent that population. The collective process is very effective in this regard. If one intervision is excelling or lagging, an analysis can be done to improve that area, or to help other areas in the organization learn from their successes or failures. Thus begins the element of effectively communicating throughout the organization.

In effect, as information is analyzed, it must be listened to and learned from at many levels:

- Company-wide
- Intervision (department, division, business unit, etc.)
- Location

It can also be listened to and learned from related to:

- Leaders and non-leaders (however you choose to define this)
- Position/role
- Age generation (Baby Boomers, Generation X, Generation Y, etc.)

There is a tremendous shift in age generation due to Baby Boomers retiring over the next several years. We have found this to be a very important category for organizations to Listen and Learn as it provides much data related to communicating more effectively with different groups.

Act

Act is another – and possibly the – key differentiator for AL^2A compared to other systems. Ask is done by organizations in many forms, although not as comprehensive as with AL^2A. Listen and Learn are often completed by leaders, but not as often as you may believe, and not by as many leaders as should be involved. And while some organizations act, we question to what extent. Action takes many forms and most are minimal. Graphic 6.2 provides a description of how all elements of AL^2A work together with People.

Act should take the form of a detailed action plan. It should be in SMART format – Specific, Measurable, Attainable, Relevant, Time-Based – indicating who is responsible for what and when.[16] After reviewing information from people, organizations define action by communicating better or recruiting better people. These are not SMART.

Act requires creating a plan, engaging people in the plan, communicating the actions in the plan, and executing the plan.[17] It requires engaging *all* leaders in the communication so they have a clear understanding of the Listen and Learn phase. It requires working with the leaders to help them cascade the information throughout the organization to their people. Once the SMART actions are determined, it requires creating cross-functional teams of people – leaders and non-leaders – to implement the actions. This truly engages people into AL^2A.

While this represents the beginning of Act, doing so through a comprehensive Performance Management system is discussed in more detail in Chapter 7. This chapter concludes with two People In Action stories to further illustrate the effectiveness of AL^{2}A.

Graphic 6.2: AL^{2}A with People

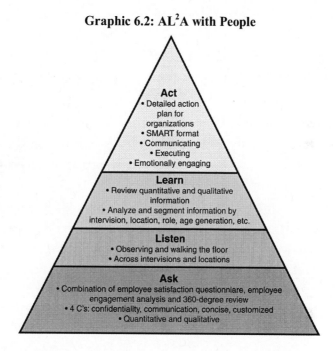

People In Action

A $50 million consulting and engineering solutions firm used the AL^{2}A process and discovered its people wanted a leadership development program. The firm already had a leadership development program. They learned the program obviously had not been effectively communicated, and those that were aware of it, did not understand it because the program was too confusing.

This supports pay not being the primary benefit people seek. If pay were the number one benefit, the people of this firm may have indicated they wanted more. Higher pay is not an easy request for an organization to fulfill as it is obviously expensive. A leadership development program also has some associated expenses – people and resources must be allocated for training and mentoring. The difference is the long-term benefit for the organization for their investment in a leadership development program as opposed to simply paying people more. Viewing leadership development as an investment – not an expense.

Leadership created a cross-functional team comprised of next generation leaders from various geographic locations and intervisions. The team began with a review of the current leadership development program, made revisions to it based on feedback from others, piloted it, and created a communication plan to roll out the newly revised program.

Fortunately, for this organization, its people's long-term interests are aligned with those of the organization. By choosing to Ask, Listen and Learn from its people; this organization was able to Act by synchronizing specific needs with them.

People In Action

A relatively new regional bank with five locations in six years and assets of almost $500 million was growing at a rapid rate. Its growth was almost entirely from incremental growth, rather than acquisitions. Its business model was based on service and customer relationships, which was very important in its geographic area where local banking and personalization were very important.

Leadership decided to partake in AL^2A, even though there were no apparent people issues. Leadership believed they knew employees' needs despite the fact they had never been formally asked since the bank's formation. Overall AL^2A ratings were extremely high as "Would you recommend Company X as a place to work to friends or colleagues?" rated a 6.59 (on a scale of 7.0) and the lowest rating was a 5.22 (which is very high for a low rating). Several recommendations were made related to improving communications, broadening marketing efforts, and creating and/or improving the current employee recognition and training programs. With its foundation of service and relationships, the bank was built on removing hierarchical organizational levels so people had autonomy to be proactive and make quick decisions for their customers. Yet, leadership found this wasn't occurring effectively in some locations. Training people on this also needed improvement.

A SMART action plan was created based on these recommendations, and people from all locations were engaged. Leadership views this as a positive step to its continued growth goals, as they base these goals on their people.

Concluding Thoughts

The AL^2A process is all in the name of strategy. You may recall aligning intervisions or locations as a key outcome of the entire strategic process. AL^2A gives you an idea of how people feel about their role in the organization, and if they are as engaged as others. People will tell you if they are aligned or not. This is crucial information as you move forward in your strategic efforts to align all areas of your organization.

Chapter 6: Summary

■ AL^{2}A (Ask, Listen, Learn & Act) is a newly created process that provides organizations with an opportunity to assess your people's and customers' current reality. It provides the bookends related to People and Customers that surround your overall strategy.

■ People in an organization should be emotionally engaged. This is superior to employee satisfaction and even employee engagement.

■ The Ask part of AL^{2}A consists of employee satisfaction, employee engagement and a 360-degree review.

■ AL^{2}A is based on four key assumptions – the 4 C's of confidentiality, communication, concise and customized.

■ Customization and/or personalization is a key differentiator of AL^{2}A as every organization and its people are different.

■ Act is a key differentiator of AL^{2}A as action must be done in SMART format and be properly executed. The Act process is similar to what you should do with your strategic plan – the same should be done as part of AL^{2}A. While Strategy, People and Customers represent a puzzle, each piece of the puzzle is completed with an AL^{2}A puzzle of its own.

■ What did you learn from the People In Action?

Chapter 7

Communication and Performance Management

"In order to succeed, you must know what you are doing,
like what you are doing,
and believe in what you are doing."
– Will Rogers

Leading people would be easy if every person in your organization were committed to the success of the organization. People willing to do more for less – emotionally engaged people. These people truly believe in what they are doing. They buy into the objective of the organization and have a clear understanding of the objective. There is a simple way to enhance your people's understanding of this. You must effectively communicate with them.

It seems like a basic concept. Yet, communication – especially in our electronic age – is vast. Communication is a main component to the Act phase of AL²A. Organizations that say they act; however, are unable to effectively communicate, will not be successful. To fully achieve Act and complete AL²A, your organization needs a Performance Management system.

Communication

In its most raw form, communication is a five-step process:
1. A sender creates a message.
2. The message is transmitted through a channel.
3. The message is received.
4. The message is interpreted.
5. The message is acted upon (responded to, understood, disregarded, etc.

In most cases, Step 1 of the process – creating a message – is simple. With varying degrees of success, messages are created all the time. Even the worst messages – those that are incomprehensible, senseless or just plain rude – illicit some response; possibly a blank stare or worse, depending on the mood that day. Messages pertaining to organizations are many of the things previously mentioned – such as the main objective. Section I focused on how to develop an effective objective, one that really incorporates the other value-based pieces: mission and vision. You are able to create an objective, which takes us to step 2 of communication. What channel is used to communicate it?

Communication Gaps

In our experiences, communication is typically the number one gap troubling people. It is the missing link per se in these organizations. Regardless of how well it is done, people always seem to want it done better. Research also shows specifically where people want key messages to come from.[1] Though people expect some input from an organization's top leader – the president or CEO – people really want communication with their direct leader.

Based on our research, lack of communication from a direct leader has become a main reason people leave an organization.[2] Typically, an issue will arise between people and their leader, and it is the lack of, or poor communication, that leads to departure. This comes back to the step 2 of communication: "The message is transmitted through a channel." In this case, the channel is a person – the direct leader.

The repercussions of people leaving – turnover – for any reason have been previously pointed out. It is especially damaging if A or B people are leaving. People are willing and capable of doing the work, yet are constantly at odds with their leaders due to poor communication.

> In our experiences with organizations, communication is typically the number one gap troubling people. It is the missing link in these organizations.

Internal Branding

The process of improving organizational communication begins at the top. There is a group of items all people must grasp to understand "Who we are as an organization."

- All people should know and have an understanding of the main objective (or mission/vision) of their organization.
- People must understand the organization's brand positioning. What is our target market? How do we represent our organization to our target markets?
- People must understand the message(s) the organization is communicating. Why should people do business with us?

People are evangelists for your organization. If they know and understand these items, they are your best recruiters and best salespeople without giving it a second thought.

Your people's interactions with the public are often brief. What is said in that time may have an impact on the public's perception of your organization. In the U.S. especially, many have a tendency to start conversations bluntly and to the point. Often, with a question we have all faced: *"What do you do?"* This can be overwhelming to explain in a short time.

The short time period is really like the length of an elevator ride; somewhere between 30 seconds to one minute. Your organization should have a positioning statement, or "elevator story," that your people understand. This should capture each of the items above (objective, brand and messages).

If your people don't know who you are, how can they truly be as productive as you want them to be with your customers to achieve the goals that you want? The way the system should work is, if I talk to any person in any organization at any level and ask who is your company and what do they do, the response should be pretty close to what the president would say.

People In Action

A more than $20 billion global leader in Internet networking provides its people with stock as part of their 401(k) – as a match for what people are willing to contribute to personal savings. Upon visiting the facility, we were overwhelmed with the interest people had with the firm's stock price. At the time of the visit, almost every person we observed had the firm's intranet site up with the stock ticker on their computer screen. The stock price had an obvious reciprocal effect. People wanted the stock price to go up – good for them – and in turn, they were willing to work hard to raise the stock price – good for the organization.

Another incentive was a company clothing purchase program. People were able to make clothing purchases, though, in many instances, they were entitled to clothing as part of their wellness program or as another reward. On a quarterly

> An "elevator story" is a concise statement summarizing your organization's objective, brand and message(s). People in your organization should be able to recite it in the length of an elevator ride.

basis, some leaders would distribute clothing to their people. When approached in public and asked about their organization – identified by their clothing – outsiders were curious about what the people did. This organization has done an excellent job of internal branding. When approached, people are in a position to provide the organization's elevator story – the brief synopsis that summarizes objective, brand and messaging.

This illustrates some examples of how to create emotional engagement with your people. This organization's people are clearly evangelists and help promote the organization to the community and other touchpoints.

People: Your Best Recruiters and Salespeople

Examples in the previous People In Action illustrate how people are your best recruiters and salespeople without really going out of their way. The combination of passion for what they do and the ability to concisely define their organization's positioning, makes people the best recruiters and salespeople you have.

There are other people-based ways to recruit. Providing incentives for your people to recruit others they know is an effective screening process. Rewards should increase incrementally with role value: C roles worth a $250 - $500 bonus, B roles worth a $750 - $1,000 bonus, and A roles worth up to a $2,500 bonus. When compared to the cost of hiring people through public means such as recruiting agencies, print or Internet advertising; the cost can be much more than $100,000 for leadership positions. The most expensive searches sometimes require professional recruiters, which cost up to 40 percent of base salary. Having your own recruiters in-house, your people, is a way to offset these expenses and create a more engaged workplace.

Besides the cost savings, a major benefit of people-based recruiting is the naturally occurring screening process. People serve as a reference, usually an honest and up-front one. Assuming the communication of your organization's values – the positioning – is in place, your people are well informed and know what the organization stands for. This puts them in a position to recruit prospects they feel are in line with your organization and its open roles. What an unbelievable way to save your organization's most precious resources – time and money. All made possible, not by more work, by better communication aligned with your strategy.

Communication Venues

People communication is undeniably important, certainly when the repercussions of executing it poorly are considered (i.e., turnover and misalignment).

If we take a step back and look closer at our five steps of communication, the second and third – *the message is transmitted through a channel,* followed by *the message being received* – pertain more to the venue or media which messages are transmitted.

More and more organizations have paperless communication systems. This includes e-mail, intranet, webcasts, and even videos playing on continuous loops in break rooms and on manufacturing plant floors. The key to any of these is that there is a communication channel and the messages are received. An important question to ask when choosing a channel is: "Will anyone actually receive it?"

In addition, "will they read it?" Many people receive 50 to 100+ e-mails daily and it is difficult to determine which to read with this communication overload. Creating a communication process and educating people on it is important to success. People need to understand which items to read and when.

If a video plays in the break room, will people watch it? Similar to e-mails, it is a shame to waste marketing dollars on ineffective advertising; just as it is a shame to waste time, effort and dollars on ineffective internal communication. The most effective communication channels must be carefully considered in either situation.

An intranet site can be an effective tool for communicating across your organization. Occasionally, we see intranet sites that are limited. They may be limited to Human Resource-related items such as downloadable forms or files. This is a good start, yet the intranet site should also provide organization-related communication. The positioning statement is an item to make an intranet site more of an educational piece for your people. Having the positioning statement and main objective at the top of the intranet's home page is a way to approach this; however, a statement or video clip from the president *explaining* why this is important may be more effective.

Including updates on new customers is a way to get people excited about the growth of the organization. Generally, it is refreshing for people to be first to know the achievements of the organization. They are, after all, the people contributing to the organization's success. Your people are entitled to know the customers they will be directly or indirectly affecting in the future.

Internally, keeping people in the loop about news and improvements at other locations, or if you are an international firm, news about your global markets, is an engagement tool. Sharing success stories and tactics that have worked for others are positive examples for all people and a great way to build morale. Essentially, an intranet site can be personalized to how you feel you will reach most of your people. And this is the key point – to reach the most people. Personalization increases the likelihood communication is received (back to step 3 of our communication process).

E-mail, videos, intranet or any other electronic media are excellent channels of communication for people in many organizations. There are some environments where e-mail or intranet is just not possible. For example, not everyone in some organizations has access to a computer. Some may not have the computer literacy to access the message, so it becomes an ineffective channel. In instances where electronic methods do not work, a print newsletter or a paycheck stuffer, personalized by the president, is a fine alternative. Shorter messages are excellent as paycheck stuffers.

> E-mail, videos, intranet or any other electronic media are excellent channels of communication for people in many organizations.

Don't Shoot the Messenger

In many situations, how effective a message is going to be may very well be determined by who is actually delivering it. When deciding the venue, it is just as important to identify the people a message is best delivered by. Is the president the ideal touchpoint for people in the first place?

The president should have consistent communication with all the organization's people. It becomes more difficult as the size of an organization increases; regardless, the president should communicate across the organization at least quarterly.

Granted, in today's global economy, with locations worldwide, the opportunity to communicate in person is often limited. However, this negative can easily be turned into a positive. A Webinar – an online presentation – is an option. Even if it is not shown to all people, if it is passed down the leadership ranks, at least a consistent message – starting at the top – is communicated. This ensures people are getting the president's message, and having direction provided by their leader. By doing this, the main issues related to organizational communication should be overcome: a lack of top down direction to all people and a lack of communication with direct leaders.

> Organizations should have consistent communication to all people as often as possible.

Managing Performance

Performance management ensures step 4 of the communication process – *the message is interpreted* – is occurring properly. Performance management allows your people to offer feedback regarding the effectiveness of your communication. Performance management actually takes care of steps 4 and 5 – *the message is responded to*. If your message is properly created, received and interpreted; and if you are allowing your people the opportunity to offer feedback, then the process is complete. The entire communication process allows you to take the complexities of communication and break it down into basic parts to implement an effective communication strategy.

The AL^2A process of Ask, Listen, Learn and Act is a process to assess your people's and customers' current reality. It provides the bookends related to People and Customers that surround your overall strategy. It also helps gain your people's perspectives on the communication methods they feel will work best.

As you come to the Act phase of the process, you will have an understanding of what your people's needs are and will have identified gaps in the organization. Based on this knowledge, you will have created your action plan, as well as a communication plan for Act. As part of your communication plan, take your organization to task – possibly your own personal performance – and initiate a Performance Management System. This measures how your strategies are working.

A Performance Management System is a comprehensive system for helping organizations know their strategies are being delivered consistently and executed with competence. Specifically, performance management works in conjunction with people's needs by aligning organizational goals and priorities with individual objectives for a line-of-sight measurement system.

> Performance management helps organizations know their strategies are being delivered consistently and executed with competence.

This system should be personalized and designed to electronically link people's objectives with those of the organization and strategy. The result is a performance management system where people know how they impact the bottom line and main objective.

Experience indicates that performance management leads to increased business results, providing linkage between strategy, people and customers. This linkage is synonymous with communication. If people are properly communicated with – using performance management as a tool – the result is effective linkage.

Engaged People, Aligned Intervisions, Successful Organizations

Sometimes, the most difficult part of some people's job is not the actual work. It is going to work every day not knowing how their work – or tasks – contributes to the bottom line of the organization.

Organizational leaders must encourage emotionally engaged people behavior by reinforcing how the work impacts the organization. By understanding people's contributions to the organization, they are more productive. AL^2A achieves this by Asking, Listening, Learning and Acting.

The next step is helping people appreciate their job as a vital part of life and truly emotionally engaging them with the organization. This should not be misunderstood as a lack of balance. Work should not take precedence over family and health. However, with the long hours spent working, it should be a positive and productive situation. This means making work important to people emotionally. This is done by giving people an opportunity to use their strengths in order to achieve their individual goals as well as intervision and company goals. This line-of-sight perspective enables people to see how their actions affect the bottom line of the organization and main objective.

Beyond annual reviews and vague individual objectives, best practice organizations continually strive to measure increases in productivity with their revenue growth and business goals. Studies consistently demonstrate that setting specific corporate goals improves productivity – sometimes as much as 30 percent.[3] The key is to effectively link corporate goals with individual goals so people understand their impact on the bottom line and how they help achieve the main objective. When done, your organization will have all the pieces of a puzzle to gain a competitive advantage.

High-performing firms that do this effectively have developed a process for sharing and monitoring organizational goals with people objectives. This process is referred to as a Performance Management System. Performance management ensures that organizations are aligned from top to bottom, and working together in an optimum manner to achieve an organization's desired results. This includes critical processes, intervisions and people.

People are a critical function of a performance management system as they are the most important representatives of your brand – your brand evangelists. Engaged people effectively help market your brand to customers and also can become your best HR recruiters for new people. They can become corporate ambassadors, and believe it or not, money is not their primary motivator.

Of course, the only way to truly know is to ask. Items such as recognition, training, career advancement, and learning new things always rank higher for people motivations.[4] If people are engaged and aligned in your organization, and have a clear understanding of your corporate goals and how they can impact these goals, their level of productivity increases. They treat customers better (customers sense when people are happy), complete customer satisfaction and loyalty occur, and the result is more growth for your organization.

Yes, this sounds simple, and it is. People continue to rank very high on items of importance for CEOs and organizational leaders. Yet, in our experiences, only a handful truly has a comprehensive performance management system in place.

Structure, Placement, Performance, Development, Reward

As it has been discussed that performance management relates to individuals and the organization, Graphic 7.1[5] explains how this occurs.

Graphic 7.1: Performance Management
for the Organization & Individuals

Structure	Placement	Performance	Development	Reward
For the organization: What is necessary for an organization to achieve its objectives?				
Create a strategic plan that aligns the main objective with goals, strategies and tactics.	Identify the right roles. And then, follow the 4 R's of recruiting, retraining, rewarding and retention.	Align individual people goals to priorities, responsibilities and skills; and stimulate performance improvement.	Provide the training, development, and growth (through coaching) necessary to achieve success.	Provide the rewards and recognition necessary to retain and motivate people.
Apply AL²A and other processes to ensure organizational success.	Identify and take advantage of the opportunities and experiences necessary for my career advancement.	Understand what I must do to be successful, how well I am doing, and what I must do to improve.	Acquire the training, development, and growth for necessary advancement opportunities.	Earn the rewards and recognition I deserve.
For the indivdual: What is necessary to enable individuals to achieve their potential?				

For the organization, it begins with a clear structure which has been discussed in Section I – related to Strategy. This flows to placement of people in terms of items discussed in Chapter 5 – identifying the right roles and accomplishing the 4 R's of recruiting, retraining, rewarding and retention. Performance is next as the organization needs to align the individual people's goals, strengths and skills with the roles. The organization then looks to develop people through training and coaching, leading to rewards and recognition.

The process is the same for people, although they begin with rewards and work toward structure. Rewards and recognition are typically high on the list of items people want[6] – not compensation. Their rewards should be based on development and career advancement opportunities, stemming from their performance. They trust the organization to place them in roles to be successful, playing to their strengths and skills; and to have the appropriate structure and process to effectively Ask, Listen, Learn and Act (AL^2A).

While Graphic 7.1 may appear complex, it is relatively simple if broken into individual steps and communicated effectively. In our experiences, once set up in an organization and people are proactively educated and trained, the process becomes simple.

People In Action

In Chapter 5, we discussed a global $1 billion provider of innovative identification solutions. Its bench strength process directly relates to performance management. While this organization has a performance management system and advancement opportunities for all people, let's focus on performance management for its top performers. Acquisitions are a core part of their strategy. Their plan is communicated to people each quarter via various communication vehicles, and each month, a key goal in the plan (e.g., acquisitions) is discussed in detail. People know the strategic plan and corporate goals, and understand them.

Each month, the leadership team meets for up to four hours to discuss top performing people. They have more than 6,000 people globally, and through their detailed process, they have identified approximately 60 people – less than 1 percent – as being the best of the best. This group of 60 knows they are on this list and the people, HR and leadership have collaborated on specific skills and training for these individuals.

When an acquisition occurs, the leadership team determines the 3-4 people that may best be qualified to lead the respective acquisition process – participating in due diligence and leading integration efforts. These people already know they will be requested to do this as they understand the importance of acquisitions to the corporate goals. These people interview for the role and one is selected to lead the acquisition efforts. This also becomes a core component of their individual leadership development program.

In this instance, this organization was focused on linking acquisitions to development. To help with their success, the Integration Leaders requested a detailed Acquisition and Integration Process Guide, which served to educate all people on the acquisition process – so acquisitions became process-dependent and not people-dependent. This also works as a career advancement opportunity for the selected acquisition leader. The company understands the importance in investing in tools to help its people succeed. The result, in addition to successful acquisition and integration efforts, is complete linkage from people, to departments/intervisions, to corporate goals.

How the Process Works

Viewed another way, a performance management system consists of a complete process of the following:

Strategic Plan: You must have a strategic plan and it must be communicated – along with the SMART corporate goals – to all people. In addition, the strategy must be continuously reviewed.

Intervision Goals: Once corporate goals are determined, these should be linked to each intervision. For example, if a corporate goal is to introduce a new product, the marketing intervision ultimately may be responsible for this. The marketing leader will make this corporate goal a part of his/her intervision goals and communicate accordingly with the team of people.

People Goals: Using the new product example, 1 or 2 individual people may be responsible for leading the new product objective. This becomes part of their annual review, thus creating a line-of-sight process from the people to the intervision/department to the corporate goals in the strategic plan.

Two other necessary components for success include measurement and communication. **Measurement** is the foundation for the system as it is the method to effectively track and determine people's needs and if/how they are impacting the bottom line. This can be accomplished in a variety of ways, mainly through AL^2A. This is where the 360-

> Performance management consists of five core items: strategic plan, intervision goals, people goals, measurement and communication.

degree assessment works best. Because it is based on an individual's feedback, as well as peers, leader and direct report (if applicable); it forms a comprehensive view of the person. This becomes the basis of their individual training and development plan.

Communication becomes the final step in the process. A comprehensive communication plan should encompass the process and ensure that information is cascaded to all people through a variety of previously discussed venues. If people don't understand what is occurring in the organization, how can they truly be as productive as you want them to be to achieve your organizational goals, maximizing productivity and profitability?

Graphic 7.2 shows the alignment from the main objective to the annual goals in the strategic plan. Intervision goals relate to the corporate annual goals, and once defined, flow to individual goals. While measurement and communication are not shown in this graphic, the entire process is two-way as individuals should not simply be fed their goals (a one-way arrow). The arrows go both ways as the process is a *give and take*, a two-way process between the individual and the intervision.

Graphic 7.2: Performance Management System

Ongoing Commitment

To ensure success, the system needs to occur on a continuous basis. There needs to be a constant communication loop between the corporate strategy, intervisions and people. A corporate scorecard should be created with the corporate goals (see Graphic 7.3). As part of the communication, the measurement should be tracked using a simple green, yellow and red light so people know which corporate goals are accomplished and which aren't. When linked to individual goals, these goals use a similar green, yellow and red system so people always know how they are performing. The alignment is completed as all people now know how they are contributing to the bottom line.

Communication helps circulate the information on strategy, goals and the main objective to leaders, intervisions and people. Remember that people are your best salespeople, recruiters and brand evangelists, so over-communicate if necessary. If over-communicating, this should only be important information so people are not overwhelmed with unnecessary items – information overload.

> It is the responsibility of leaders to proactively communicate with people. People should never be surprised at how they are doing.

To realize a strong communication strategy, communication must continually cascade. Leaders must be open and honest with their teams of people whether they are helping to further the company objective or eroding it. People should always know how they are performing. If a person goes in to get an annual assessment, there should never be a surprise. If this individual walks out surprised, that tells us that there is no, or at least a lack of communication between the leader and the person. The responsibility is on the leader – not the person – to proactively communicate.

This process must be ongoing. If you communicate to someone how they are doing today, don't think you know how they are doing tomorrow or next week or next year. There needs to be a continuous communication loop.

Graphic 7.3 indicates a corporate scorecard or a dashboard of measures. By creating a frequently updated intranet site with feedback information – both positive and negative – organizations provide an easy access method to find alignment. The simple red, yellow and green light method works very well because it is visual and simple to understand. This can be done for the organization's goals, intervision's goals, and individual's goals – all with the same simple method.

Graphic 7.3: Dashboard of Measures

Aligning Jack with the Organization

Suppose that Jack is an operations worker that packages bread on a line eight hours a day. For Jack to be emotionally engaged, he must understand that without his work packaging the bread, the bread can lose moisture and become moldy. If the bread is moldy, customers will not want to buy it, and the company will lose business, resulting in potential job losses – including Jack. Jack now understands how his actions affect the organization, and furthermore how it returns to affect him.

For performance management to be effective, line of sight thinking needs to be instilled from leaders to people. Let's say the organization has a bonus system to reward individuals such as Jack. He can potentially earn a 10 percent bonus for the year. Rather than just grant him his bonus based on his individual performance, his intervision's performance, or the organizations' performance; he can earn a bonus based on the success of each these combined. Let us explain more specifically based on the 10 percent bonus:

- A typical bonus plan for an organization is to offer a 10 percent bonus to everyone in the organization if a certain goal (usually tied to revenue or profitability) is reached. Traditionally, this has been great to foster a team environment because individuals either sink or swim in regard to their bonuses, with the rest of the team. If Jack can pack an average of 100 loaves of bread daily, he will earn 4 percent of his bonus for the year. This would be one of his individual goals. At this point, we have not considered the wide-spanning organizational goals.

- Jack works on a team with five other bread-packers and a leader that sets the schedule and measures the packed loaves. If these six people – the entire team – maintain an average of packing 600 loaves daily for the entire year, each team member will be rewarded another 3 percent bonus.

- So far, if Jack and his co-workers have reached their goals, they will have a 7 percent bonus at the end of the year. Now, Jack is motivated. He has engaged in teamwork with his co-workers, and with an organization-wide bonus – another 3 percent for the revenue or profitability goal – he will have a 10 percent bonus for the year.

This example provides Jack with the line-of-sight perspective it takes to realize the long-term implications of his daily actions. Furthermore, his compensation is directly tied to these long-term actions, so he is emotionally engaged in his tasks, those of his team, and the overall organization.[7]

Concluding Thoughts

By now, you should be able to effectively create your strategy, form your main objective, know how and when to engage people and customers in creating your strategic plan, and be innovative (to an extent). You also should be able to determine the right organizational roles, along with the 4 R's; effectively utilize AL^2A; and communicate and form a performance management system.

Two-thirds of the puzzle is complete. We now turn our attention to customers.

Chapter 7: Summary

■ Communication is typically the number one gap troubling people. It is the missing link in these organizations.

■ An elevator story is a concise statement summarizing your organization's objective, brand and messages. People should be able to recite it in the length of an elevator ride. What is your elevator story?

■ Your people are your best recruiters and salespeople – they are your evangelists.

■ Use a variety of communication vehicles to achieve your strategy. Organizations should have consistent communication to all people as often as possible. Over-communicate important items only to avoid communication overload.

■ Performance management helps organizations know their strategies are being delivered consistently and executed with competence. There is a natural flow from AL^2A to performance management.

■ Structure, Placement, Performance, Development and Reward are key elements for organizations and individuals related to performance management.

■ Performance management consists of five core items: strategic plan, intervision goals, people goals, measurement and communication.

■ It is the responsibility of the leader to proactively communicate with people. People should never be surprised at how they are doing.

■ What did you learn from the People In Action?

Section III

Customers

"Motivate them, train them, care about them and make winners out of them. We know that if we treat our employees correctly, they'll treat the customers right. And if customers are treated right, they'll come back."
– J.W. Marriott, Jr.

Customers. You may be thinking, "Why has it taken so long to get to a discussion about customers?" If you recall our puzzle, you can begin with any piece – Strategy, People or Customers. Which piece you begin with varies greatly based on where you are in the evolution of your organization.

When I started my business, strategy was my first puzzle piece, then customers, then people. By the second year, I focused on people first, then customers, then strategy. Entering my third year, it was customers, then people, then strategy. This is not to say this is what every organization should do, or that people and strategy are no longer important. Remember, all three pieces need continuous attention to achieve profitability and success.

Chapter 3 discussed the chicken and the egg in determining whether to include people or customers first in strategy. As Section II dealt with people, one can conclude we believe people should first be incorporated with your strategy, and then customers.

Section III presents a chicken and the egg of its own related to customers. Which comes first – market research, brand positioning or AL^2A? The answer is similar to the puzzle in that it depends upon where your organization is at in its life cycle. A new organization should focus first on market research, then brand positioning, and then AL^2A with its best customers. A market leader may first do AL^2A, then brand positioning, then market research.

Section III focuses on finding and keeping the right customers, as well as introducing six steps to customer strategy. Chapter 8 focuses on determining the right customers and knowing your target market. Chapter 9 assumes you have done everything in Chapter 8, and relates to steps 1 through 4 of customer strategy. This involves determining all touchpoints, creating your brand and positioning, and prioritizing customers. Chapter 10 centers on step 5 of customer strategy about conducting research as a means to get to AL^2A.

Chapter 11 explains AL^2A with Customers (remember this relates to people and customers) and discusses ongoing measurement aligned with performance management (discussed in Chapter 7).

Read them in the order that is best for you and your organization. Although it is recommended to read all four chapters, as like the puzzle, regardless of where your organization's life cycle currently is, all elements needs to be continually completed or the puzzle is not effective.

Chapter 8

The Right Customers

"Listening to other companies' customers
is the best way to gain market share,
while listening to the visionaries
is the best way to create new markets."
— Karl Albrecht

The right customers are not the ones who try to bleed you dry. Determining which customers are right is an important strategy every organization should know as, inevitably, it is okay to fire customers that are wrong for your organization.

Customers should be viewed similar to people in terms of the 4 R's (discussed in Chapter 5). Customers need to be proactively recruited, retrained, rewarded and retained. Remember the other R – roles – as you need to determine the roles in which customers fit.

The 4 R's: Customers

Determining your right customers is a process. You cannot be all things to all people. Recruiting customers equates to establishing those you want to develop relationships. Profiling prospects, industries, segments, markets, etc. Knowing which person in which intervision at which location to target. This relates to demographics and psychographics, both which are discussed later in this chapter.

> To identify your distinct functional areas, we have created a new term – intervisions – or "visions together." Your intervisions work cohesively sharing the same vision; with the strategy as the means to the objective as the end.

Retraining customers seems odd; however, most organizations want to have a true relationship with their customers. We have found that partnerships flourish much more than relationships. Think of it personally… I have relationships with many people in my office; however, I have a *partnership* with my spouse. A partnership is a more meaningful bond than a customer relationship. You want to have relationships with all of your customers, and should have partnerships with a core group of your best customers. Customers need training on how to have relationships and partnerships with you.

Rewarding can mean many things varying from customer to customer. Some prefer recognition. Others prefer continually exceeding their expectations. Others prefer a day of golf. Determining their rewards comes from AL^2A.

Retaining customers – the right ones – is known to most everyone and retaining the wrong ones is not wise. This is why it is important to know the answer to the question, "How do I determine and know which customers are the right ones?"

The fifth R is Roles. Role designation begins to help determine if you have the right customers and which customers to recruit. Do you want customers to provide a great deal of volume at lower margins to have high capacity and keep people employed? Do you only want highly profitable customers? Do you want customers valuing service and willing to pay a premium?

Customers In Action

A national perishable food distributor has been growing at double digits rates during the past five years. Based on growth, the president was gaining too many customers and saw their own service declining in some areas. He decided to go through a customer selection process.

In one instance, he contacted a key, long time, loyal customer of more than 10 years. Despite this, it never paid invoices on time and was

> Customers should be viewed similar to people in terms of the 4 R's.

slow to respond when contacted. Upon speaking with the customer's president, the message was, "we're not going to do business with you anymore because you don't pay invoices on time and you are unresponsive when we contact you. We are at 100 percent of capacity and are going to be selective in who we do business with."

The result: the customer apologized and asked for another chance. They now pay invoices one week ahead of time and have a dialogue to grow business – resulting in more of a partnership.

Wal-Mart and Supplier Interactions

Another example of the 4 R's can be viewed by looking at the largest customer for many organizations. Though their flaws have made them an easy target over the years, let us examine how Wal-Mart treats its suppliers to determine if they fit into your right customer category.

Over the past decade, Wal-Mart has been able to provide many consumer goods at prices well below market. For many consumers, these prices are a blessing that has allowed them to save money and/or invest in other items. Few can argue with abundant, affordable food, clothing and household items. It is the manner in which prices are kept so low that has gained this organization negative publicity over the past few years.

Once admonished for taking over small towns, Wal-Mart has been held responsible for turning farm fields into supercenters and contributing to the deterioration of city centers. Many people have become accustomed to the takeovers; their resentment has been shifted to the organizations' poor treatment of its loyal suppliers.[1]

The retailer sets many standards for its suppliers, including ensuring supplier's prices fall, as a means to fulfill the "falling prices" promise to customers.[2] This puts continual pressure on suppliers to maintain their supply to Wal-Mart using lower cost methods, irrespective of inflation and other rising costs (e.g., fuel).

One such cost that Wal-Mart has pushed to its suppliers is the implementation of RFID – Radio Frequency Identification Technology. Widespread implementation of this technology allows Wal-Mart tremendous efficiencies and competitive advantage over retailers still using older technologies. The real bonus for Wal-Mart is the majority of the high implementation costs are being passed on to suppliers, and Wal-Mart has set a mandate that they must comply.[3]

For some suppliers, this is not an end-of-the-world crisis. High margin goods will not be as affected by the cost of a $1 to $3 RFID tag. Consider the cost of a product with a smaller margin, perhaps a pallet of pickles, which because of high quantity, may have a margin of only a few dollars. In this instance, $1 to $3 can make a significant impact on the profit of a pallet, not to mention the long-term health and sustainability of the organization.[4]

On top of other demands, Wal-Mart's bill paying procedure may be the most shrewd and harmful tactic to its suppliers. Having its shelves consistently stocked is almost as important to its business model as low prices. The expectation for a supplier is simple: Wal-Mart requires products on-time and on the shelves, end of story.[5]

Some suppliers, especially those with perishable goods, need to re-supply the retailer in less than 10 days. Coming from the world's largest retailer, this appears to be a promising volume of business. However, what would happen to a supplier, one without a huge cash-flow, if Wal-Mart, like most large organizations, only paid its bills every 30 to 60 days? That means three to six cycles of replenishing shelves, for one payment. The supplier would be cash-strapped, sometimes to a dire degree, to keep up with this cycle.

This is exactly the tactic Wal-Mart employs to achieve two things: always stocked shelves and a positive cash flow. And because of their high sales volume and supplier dependency, they can.[6]

Getting to the point of *your customers*, are customers with the greatest possible sales potential always the right customers? Well, not all of Wal-Mart's suppliers are treated like those in the previous examples. A fortunate few have become so valuable to Wal-Mart's supply chain and its goal of continuously stocked shelves, they are exempt from some of the practices previously discussed. In fact, one supplier we are aware of has proven its value to Wal-Mart beyond just another shelf-filler.

The $3.5 billion global manufacturer in the food and beverage industry we previously discussed is one of Wal-Mart's key suppliers. Because of this supplier's tremendous volume and supply chain (and with Wal-Mart, this is a lot of volume), they are actually able to leverage an equitable supplier-to-customer relationship with the retail giant – at fair margins.

Reflection on Wal-Mart

While it may be difficult for many of you to reflect on Wal-Mart as you may never do business with them for a variety of reasons, the lessons learned and questions raised relate to your own organization. Thinking of the 4 R's, all suppliers that do business with Wal-Mart have recruited them. As far as we know, Wal-Mart doesn't proactively search out suppliers they can do business with – most suppliers approach Wal-Mart.

Retraining Wal-Mart may be difficult for most organizations as Wal-Mart tends to govern the relationship. However, using the example of Wal-Mart's top suppliers, this demonstrates they do partner with and train these suppliers to achieve an effective and efficient supply chain.

Rewarding relates to the partnership with top suppliers as well. Wal-Mart may reward these suppliers by not continually pushing down their price as they value the product, service and supply chain.

Retention is a two-way street. Wal-Mart can choose which suppliers it will retain based its measurement tools. And suppliers can always choose to keep Wal-Mart as a customer. Proactively conducting the AL^2A process with a key customer like Wal-Mart helps with this.

Customers In Action

A service provider has a customer located 50 minutes from its nearest location. Services include marketing strategy, research and project execution. Revenues from the customer represent approximately 5 percent of total revenues and have been the same for three consecutive years.

The service provider has made efforts to grow the business with this customer, and the customer is frugal and chooses only to invest in the marketing efforts it feels are important. Not necessarily the same items annually; however, the same total annual budget amount. Despite this, the provider chooses to keep this customer as it epitomizes the right customer. Irregardless of limited growth opportunity, the business is relatively profitable with low demands; the contact person (Sales & Marketing vice president) is extremely responsive and easy to do business with, not to mention, he will become the next president in less than one year. They prefer electronic communication, thereby saving travel time. In addition, the contact serves as a good reference for other prospects and the current president serves on several Boards for other referral venues.

For the service provider, this customer fits a specific role as a customer that may not generate a lot of revenue; however, provides good profitability and values high quality services. During an annual meeting, each retrained the other's business, and the client has been retained.

Demographics and Psychographics

At the beginning of this chapter, demographics and psychographics were mentioned relative to recruiting and roles for customers. As you cannot be all things to all people, how do you know who to target as customers?

We will refer to a People discussion in Chapter 5 about strengths, as this correlates to Customers. Just as people have specific strengths that must be cultivated, organizations have these as well. While some have demonstrated that an organization should focus on only one thing and do it the best they can,[7] we believe it is acceptable for an organization to focus on multiple items – certainly no more than three to five based on the organization's size – similar to an individual having five core strengths.[8]

Your organization needs to go through a process of determining its strengths and/or core competencies because this will help establish what you do well, which is important to clarify the demographics and psychographics of your customers. Strengths can be done by internal reflection, assessing the current situation and AL^2A. After determining your organization's strengths, next consider the demographics of your market.

Business-to-business demographics include organization size (people and revenues), geographic region, title/role of contact person, industry, home office or satellite office, etc. Business-to-consumer demographics include gender, age range, geographic region, etc.

> Just as people have specific strengths that must be cultivated, organizations have these as well.

Often, organizations stop after considering their demographics. Unfortunately, this is not enough as psychographics are increasingly important. These relate to personality, values, interests, lifestyles, etc. Business-to-business involves risk taker vs. not risk taker, never satisfied vs. content, values quality vs. doesn't, values low cost/low service vs. doesn't, etc. Business-to-consumer may differentiate between Generation Y vs. Baby Boomers, those with health problems vs. those without, those owning a luxury vehicle vs. those without, etc.

I will illustrate using my own organization. In terms of demographics, we target companies in most industries as our services are not specific to a particular industry. We target the president, vice president of marketing, or vice president of human resources; our geographic region is global, yet we begin locally and expand incrementally in terms of targeted opportunities; and company size is those having revenues of $1 billion or less, with a more defined niche of $15 million to $500 million. Our psychographics are defined by an acronym we refer to as WIRED. These are the characteristics of the customers that choose to partner with us and with whom we choose to partner. It stands for:

- **W**isdom: To gain more knowledge
- **I**mproved Capabilities: To maximize productivity
- **R**esults: To maximize profitability
- **E**ager to Learn: To increase innovation
- **D**esire to Commit: To be successful

While WIRED has some generalities, we know these are the main descriptors of our customers. If the organization or contact person is not WIRED, we choose not to do business with them. This greatly helps with market identification efforts and avoids partnering with those not aligned with our strategy.

Demographics:	**Psychographics**:
Industry	Personality
Role in Organization (CEO, VP)	Interests
Geographic Region	Values
Company Size	Lifestyle

Growing with or without Customers

Let's briefly touch on growing and expanding your organization. This involves growing for the sake of growing; growing with your customers; or not knowing if, how or where to grow. Some questions to consider include: Do you want to be local, regional or global; or can you afford not to be regional and global?

The two main philosophies are: "We will build it and they will (hopefully) come," and "We will go where our customers go/we will follow our customers." The first involves higher risk, expanded marketing and potentially higher investment costs related to a new building, etc. The latter involves less risk as you may already have your customers' business when entering the market, so less marketing; though the costs associated with a new building or acquisition, etc. remain.

Going where your customers grow assumes you have a nimble and flexible organization to react quickly to customers. Or, from using the AL^2A process, you have incorporated your customers' strategy into your own and proactively are growing with them. This indicates having partnerships with your top customers.

> Two main philosophies are: "We will build it and they will (hopefully) come," and "We will go where our customers go."

Let's use the example of our heroic food manufacturer and their demanding customer, Wal-Mart. They faced losing market share with Wal-Mart as the retail giant expanded internationally. Could a supplier with a supply chain limited to the U.S. meet the demand at a reasonable price internationally?

Supplying customers wherever they go is subject to strategy, and strategy must be continuously reviewed as customers' needs evolve. Consider an acquisition strategy. There are existing suppliers in your customers' new market – and there is no reason you should lose business to these suppliers. An option may be to build or lease a facility in this new market. Consider if the return is worth the investment in this customer or partner, and if not yet a partner, will the investment create one.

Fortunately, the food manufacturer was proactive and already had facilities in Wal-Mart's new regions. The globalization was part of the manufacturer's overall strategy, with Wal-Mart's growth and expansion a key consideration in this strategy, and a return far exceeding the investment. As Wal-Mart expanded, they were already there. Ideally, the best strategy is to be ahead of your customers.

Customers In Action

A new bank entered a familiar market when two high-level leaders from a competing bank led the effort. Based on this, the new leaders had several local customers and partnerships, which provided a good start for their new business. Instead of growing into new markets by building new branches, they initially chose to remain local. They recruited other bankers from competitors with the hope of bringing their customers and partnerships.

Based on customer requests, leadership added another local branch. Despite competitors buying land and developing new buildings in its market and surrounding regional markets, the bank grew regionally as its strategy projected. Leadership recruited key people from regional competitors to these new locations as their business is based on customer partnerships.

The bank decided to enter another new regional market, a market that lacked prior knowledge of them. Before entering the market, a key person was hired from a competitor and a decision was made to acquire an existing building to remodel it into another new branch.

Its competitors have invested in new buildings and have spent capital. Competitor's lax hiring practices do not compare to the strategy of hiring top performers from other banks. Competitors struggled, and it showed in their financials.

This illustrates how a long-term strategy will guide you to the right markets, the right people in the right roles, and the right customers – all to gain market share while maximizing profitability.

Concluding Thoughts

Building the right customer base is not easy as it is never easy to walk away from business. This presents a difficult short-term strategy as many organizations are afraid to fire customers. Long-term, the strategy is effective as it maximizes profitability while allowing your organization to continuously review the strategy and evolve it based on customers' constantly changing needs and desires. Now that you know which customers are right, the next chapter takes you through a process of effectively positioning your organization, its products and services to your customers.

Chapter 8: Summary

- Customers should be viewed similar to people in terms of the 4 R's. They need to be proactively recruited, retrained, rewarded and retained, as well as the fifth R – roles.

- Reflect on Wal-Mart and why you may or may not want them as a customer, considering this will help with other customers.

- Demographics and psychographics must be defined to know if you have the right customers.

- Growing with your customers, or better yet, partnering with them so you can grow *ahead* of them, is a great strategy.

- You should know when to walk away from and "fire" customers.

- What did you learn from the Customers In Action?

Chapter 9

Customer Strategy Process

"It is not necessary to change.
Survival is not mandatory."
– W. Edwards Deming

This chapter describes six steps of creating a customer strategy. A key element of the strategy is to construct effective brand and message positioning. Based on this, it is necessary to discuss branding first, and then analyze the six step customer strategy.

Branding is a topic whereby much has been written and there are many organizations that *do* branding.[1] This chapter is about creating a customer strategy; and incorporating branding and integrating messages to effectively position your organization, its products and its services. Branding is not about a creative logo and making something look nice. These are components of branding, but not the process, nor the messaging.

Terminology and What Branding is Not

Before proceeding, we want to provide our definition of several branding terms, as well as explain what it is not (based on our experiences). A <u>brand strategy</u> is an emotional partnership that organizations have with everyone they touch – touchpoints. Touchpoints may include people (employees), customers, suppliers, end users, prospects, etc. It is a long-term strategy that employs policies, tools and processes to build, maintain, measure and refresh a brand's equity with its touchpoints, thereby optimizing its value. There are several key words in this definition worth discussing. Note the words emotional partnership. As people are emotionally engaged, a brand has an emotional connection with its touchpoints; and this connection is a partnership – not merely a relationship. Touchpoints are more than just customers. As people are your best salespeople and evangelists, achieving an emotional partnership with as many touchpoints as possible only broadens your sales and recruiting staff. How your organization does branding is a strategy that requires continuous review. It employs processes. You will learn of a process that achieves your customer strategy.

<u>Brand positioning</u> is the brand's messages, attributes and other marketing strategies, as well as how they are communicated and marketed to touchpoints. What is unique about your organization? What are your differentiating factors? What is your "cause"? We use brand positioning and message positioning synonymously as they both relate to the positioning of your brand, and the positioning is reflected in the messages.

<u>Brand personality</u> is the "voice" of the brand. Taking the brand positioning and giving it a life for touchpoints to feel and remember, to develop an emotional bond with it.. This is no different than your own personality. After meeting someone, how would they describe you? Entrepreneurial. Happy. Serious. Care-free. Fun. Organized. The same goes for your brand.

<u>Brand identity</u> is a set of guidelines and definitions that organizes the brands, logos and messages into a system for all

touchpoints to easily understand. This is something creative firms can do once the brand strategy, positioning and messages, and personality are achieved. It is a guide book of all items discussed thus far.

Brand equity is the set of associations and behaviors that permit the brand to earn value with touchpoints. It provides the brand with a strong, sustainable and differentiated advantage over competitors.[2]

All terminology related to your brand is similar whether it is your corporate brand or product/service brand. Each brand should have each of these items.

> Brand positioning is the brand's messages, attributes and other marketing strategies, and how they are communicated and marketed to touchpoints.

To help illustrate branding, here are items of what branding is not:

- A logo (by itself)
- A tagline (by itself)
- Something that disappears after a short time period
- Artificial or imaginary
- Focused only on external touchpoints

As the terminology mentions, a brand is much more than a creative logo and/or tagline. These are *parts* of a brand; however, not *the* brand. A brand that disappears in a short time period was not a very good brand; therefore, we deem it not a brand at all. A brand should be sustainable (consider Coca Cola's New Coke and its inability to never become "Old Coke"). A brand must be real, and it must focus on *all* touchpoints – not just customers.

Customer Strategy Process: Steps 1 - 3

Our research and experiences indicate a six step process is necessary to achieve an effective customer strategy with brand and message positioning (see Graphic 9.1). The six steps encompass much more than brand and message positioning, they provide you with a comprehensive process to follow for your entire customer strategy – attraction and retention. The final two steps are discussed in more detail in Chapters 10 and 11 as the process becomes extended into AL^2A and your performance management system.

Step 1 is to take a step back, which is needed before taking several steps forward. It is to **assess the current situation**. This should be similar to your continuous review strategic planning as there are a series of questions associated with it. In its most general form, the question to ask is: Where are we today?
Other questions include:

- Do we have the right strategy in place?
- Do we have the right people in place?
- Are we looking at the right customers?
- What are our goals?
- What secondary data is available to compare performance against success measures?

> There is a six step process to achieve an effective customer strategy with brand and message positioning.

- What critical issues are we currently facing and expect to face over the next several years?
- Do we know our customers' current and future needs?
- Do we have the right capabilities and processes to serve our market now and in the future?
- How are we performing in these processes?

These represent some of the main questions, and as these are discussed, natural off-shoot questions arise. If you can't answer these questions, it's difficult to figure out what you're going to do next. This step is about gaining internal alignment to ensure if you really have the right elements in place to move forward with the customer strategy you are forming.

Graphic 9.1: Customer Strategy Process

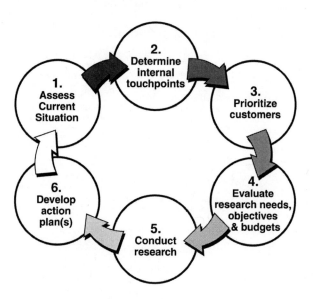

Step 2 is to **determine internal touchpoints**. This relates to internal branding. Involve key internal stakeholders from different interversions, bring these people together and ask their perceptions of your brand. While this effort may be led by marketing people, the effort should include people from all interversions as in some way, shape or form; they all touch the brand. Many people identify the attributes that establish the brand.

This step also includes engaging other touchpoints such as suppliers, community representatives, and possibly key customers. Think of this as a focus group, brainstorming session, or even type of innovation session. The facilitator – possibly external – asks questions about touchpoints' perceptions about your brand. At this time, this is not hard core, scientific research (this comes later). You are conducting internal research to ask, "How do our key stakeholders perceive us? Does it agree with how we perceive ourselves? Does it align with what our customer and brand strategy may be? Is there misalignment?

These questions and discussion provide a baseline for future steps. Even if everything you hear is completely aligned with current perceptions and strategy, more needs to be done as your market is more than a group of touchpoints sitting in a room.

Step 3 is to **prioritize customers**. Prioritizing customers is a deeper dive as it provides a more detailed analysis and review of your most valuable customers. The assumption is that you have the right customers. While all can be engaged in the process, the time and effort may yield a lower ROI. By prioritizing customers, organizations can generate the same or even better information.

Prioritization can take many forms. Some organizations use the simple 80/20 rule and prioritize the top 20 percent of their customers generating 80 percent of their revenue. Do all of these customers generate strong profitability? Does this represent a good cross-section of your customers? Is this too many or too few customers?

Another method is to prioritize based on profitability. Using the 80/20 rule, who are your most profitable customers? This can be useful as some may not be those generating the most revenue. This presents an opportunity for you to determine which customers with which to build partnerships.

A third method is to prioritize based on geographic area or industry – either by revenue or profitability – to have a good cross-section of customers.

Most organizations we are familiar with take the "easy" method of 80/20 by revenue.

As Graphic 9.2 shows, the recommendation is to take a combination of all methods and prioritize customers based on

> By prioritizing customers, organizations are able to generate the same or even better information, which transcends to all customers.

revenue (your top 5-10 customers), profitability (your top 5-10), and by geographic area or industry (another 5-10).

Graphic 9.2: Prioritized Customers Based on Total Customers

Total Customers	Revenue	Profitability	Geography/Industry	Prioritized Customers
201 or more (2 + global regions)	10/region	10/region	10 - 20/region	30 - 40/region
201 or more (1 global region)	10	10	10 - 20	30 - 40
100 - 200	5	5	5 - 10	15 - 20
<100	1 - 4	1 - 4	1 - 2	5 - 10

As a general rule, if you have 100-200 customers, choose five in each category; and if you have more than 200 customers, choose up to 10 per category. A maximum of 40 for large geographic regions such as North America, Latin America, Asia Pacific and Europe is enough. Global organizations should do this process in each of these four regions for a maximum of 40 per global region. Small and mid-sized companies with fewer than 100 customers should focus on a combination of profitability and revenue customers, choosing 5-10 total based on the total number of customers.

Prioritizing customers is an important step here because it expands on step 2 – and we will soon explain what to do with these customers. If you have not yet determined the right customers, it provides a venue to do this as well, as the prioritization makes you think long and hard about customers you currently do business with.

Customers In Action

While Net Promoter Score[3] (NPS) – a statistical measure to gauge customer loyalty – will be discussed in more detail in Chapter 10, we are familiar with one Fortune 10 firm[4] that has been doing NPS for more than 18 months. For the initial 9+ months, at least one division[5] conducted NPS with all customers, which is thousands. They then realized they needed to stop doing this and prioritize which customers they would proceed with. Without a process, it wasn't clear to them to prioritize initially.

A $300 million national packaging and printing specialist faced a similar situation. They were looking to engage customers, which included more than 1,800 customers. Through a detailed prioritization session, this was reduced to 40 key customers across the U.S. – 10 in each region (West, Midwest, South and East) based on a combination of revenues and profitability. This provided a much more manageable number than 1,800, which seemed overwhelming to them.

These examples provide illustration of the importance of prioritizing key customers. The result is to not be overwhelmed by the process of interacting with customers, while collaborating with key customers to gain information to help drive business decisions.

Customer Strategy Process: Step 4

Step 4 is to **evaluate research needs, objectives and budgets**. Here is where you take information and data gathered from steps 1 – 3 and decide what to do next. In step 2, you may have had an internal person facilitate the meeting and discussion with internal touchpoints, or you may have chosen to use an external facilitator. After step 2, you have only gathered high-level information from an important, yet small, group of stakeholders in a qualitative manner.

Having just prioritized customers, you want to go through a more detailed process with them. We recommend partnering with external experts as they can be more objective and typically do not have any preconceived notions about your brand and customers. We have also found customers (and other internal touchpoints) to be more honest with independent third party groups; regardless of how strong the organization-customer partnership may be.[6]

During this step, while evaluating research needs, many organizations determine they don't need to do further research with customers or touchpoints, or they don't have the budget for it, yet must proceed with the strategy. One of the biggest issues we see and hear is organizations do not invest in research because it is viewed as a cost instead of an investment

> Engage external experts into your process as they can be more objective and do not have preconceived notions about your brand and customers.

since nothing is ever done with the research. Organizations invest the time and money to do research, but then it just sits on a shelf somewhere – never to be used or communicated.

The next time there is a need for research, everybody says, "We invested in it the last time and it did nothing for us." This is why it is important to really evaluate your needs and objectives.

Another issue is when organizations feel it is okay to skip the research step because they conducted research several years ago and consider it still valid. Additionally, the internal people know customers' perceptions and do not need to ask them.

Your customers and the market continuously change, and your strategy must be flexible and change as well. Even in slow moving industries, conducting some type of research with customers on their brand and message perceptions is a worthwhile investment – even if it only validates what occurred years ago. This is the same rationale for knowing your customers' perceptions.[7] Worst case, you can validate what you *think* you know. If you are right, you can prove to others how smart you are. If not, you can prove to others how wise you are to have done the research.

A final issue is organizations that say they cannot afford to do research due to a limited budget that must be spent on the tactics in the marketing plan. What good are the tactics if you do not have good research to support the brand image, messages and positioning you are trying to communicate? This is difficult to understand. The investment in the research can make the tactics all the more effective, resulting in increased revenue and profitability.

We offer two brief examples demonstrating the importance of evaluating research needs, objective and budgets. First, a $3 million regional lawn, garden and landscaping firm had no growth for three consecutive years. Its leaders believed their brand and marketing strategy was the main reason, yet initially balked at investing 20 percent of their limited budget in research to determine their brand and positioning. Leaders choose to continue to invest 100 percent of their budget in tactics they did not believe were working. Upon reflection, they proceeded with the research.[8]

A second example is a $4 million regional IT firm that was investing 100 percent of its budget on radio advertising. Revenues were actually declining and its leaders were considering continuing with the radio advertising. They had never conducted research to know if this was the proper venue, and more importantly, didn't know if they were communicating their brand and positioning as they did not have this clearly defined. They decided to invest 15 percent of their limited budget in research and a marketing plan. The result: revenues grew by 20 percent in 18 months.

Customers In Action

A Fortune 200 global manufacturer of automation, control and information solutions faced a brand and message dilemma. The main corporate headquarters was serving as a holding company and had acquired four global firms over a short time period. As there was brand equity in all five brands – holding company and four acquired companies – it needed a comprehensive strategy.

Initially, leadership wanted to go to market as one brand and remove the four acquired global brands. Three of the four brands were more than 80 years old, while the fourth was less than five years old. Each of the four brands also represented a completely different product segment. Instead of making a quick, internally based decision on the brand and products, leadership chose to take a step back and assess the situation, thereby beginning the Customer Strategy Process.

In assessing the situation (step 1), they asked, "How do we position five brands in the global market?" In step 2, they formed a global marketing committee comprised of intervision leaders from around the world. In step 3, they prioritized customers. As part of step 4, they conducted a competitive analysis to determine how their main competition positioned themselves in the market and what their messages were. This caused further reflection in assessing core competencies and strengths of the five brands as each was unique.

The conclusion was to keep all five brands, yet they still needed to understand how they would function together. They knew consistency and alignment among the brands with all touchpoints was needed, but how?

They implemented steps 5 and 6 (discussed in Chapters 10 and 11) in each global region – Asia, Europe, North America and Latin America – as each of the five brands may have different messages based on the localized region. Ultimately, a comprehensive global brand strategy was created whereby the four acquired brands became product brands and were always aligned with the main corporate brand. A complete and consistent set of messages was created, allowing for flexibility by product brand and global region.

The result: the organization was chosen as one of the top five in the nation in brand management and integrated marketing communications; and upon seeing two salespeople at a conference years later, in less than one minute, both were able to sketch and explain the strategy to me.

Quantitative or Qualitative Research

As part of Step 4, there must be a detailed analysis of all of the types of research – qualitative and quantitative. In simplest terms, quantitative research is more about specific numbers related to the what, where and when of research. Qualitative research is more about a deeper understanding behind the numbers to determine the why and how of research.[9]

We recommend doing a combination of both quantitative and qualitative. There is a time and place where one is more useful than the other, and this varies greatly based on your overall research objectives. Best practice organizations should use both during the course of a year, depending upon the situation

> Organizations should consider both quantitative and qualitative research. Ultimately, use both.

and need. For our discussion, utilizing both tends to be best, which is why we have created the AL^2A process with Customers to incorporate them. This will be discussed in more detail in Chapters 10 and 11, along with steps 5 and 6 of the Customer Strategy Process.

Chapter 9: Summary

■ Be knowledgeable about each of the branding terms: brand strategy, brand positioning, brand personality, brand identity and brand equity.

■ Follow the six-step process to achieve an effective customer strategy with brand and message positioning.

■ The six steps are:
  • Assess the current situation
  • Determine internal touchpoints
  • Prioritize customers
  • Evaluate research needs, objectives and budgets
  • Conduct formal vs. informal research
  • Develop action plan(s)

■ Customers and other internal touchpoints are more open and honest with independent third party groups, regardless of how strong the organization-customer partnership is.

■ Conducting some type of research with customers about their brand and message perceptions is a worthwhile investment.

■ Do a combination of both quantitative and qualitative research to be most effective.

■ What did you learn from the Customers In Action?

Chapter 10

Getting to AL²A

"Always do right. This will gratify some people and astonish the rest."
– Mark Twain

Chapter 6 discussed AL²A (Ask, Listen, Learn & Act) with People. We have noted throughout that AL²A can also be used with customers, which is what makes it such a useful process. While the process is consistent, AL²A with Customers as opposed to people has different elements.

Chapter 11 explains the AL²A process with Customers, while this chapter reviews current options for step 5 of the Customer Strategy Process, conducting research. This helps illustrate how AL²A was developed as a process for customers and how it flows to step 6, creating action plans.

Referring to Graphic 10.1, step 5, **conduct research**, is an important part of the Customer Strategy Process as it provides baseline and ongoing measurement for your brand and message strategy, as well as your growth and performance goals. We will focus on two main types of research that are important to the success of your organization.

Types of Research

The first type of research relates to your <u>brand and message</u> <u>strategy</u>. These are key words, phrases, attributes, etc. that comprise your brand strategy, brand positioning and brand personality. These are items you want all touchpoints to think when discussing your brand, assuming you have done a great job communicating them. These must continually be measured to gauge if they are changing based on your marketing and business strategy. Do your touchpoints understand the words, phrases and attributes? Is their level of understanding increasing or decreasing? Like an approval rating for a U.S. president, this is continually tracked and measured.

Graphic 10.1: Customer Strategy Process

The second type of research is to measure your <u>growth and</u> <u>performance goals</u>. Graphic 10.2 illustrates these goals. They involve the main goals of your strategy. In Section I, you created your strategy and strategic plan. This began with your main objective and flowed to your goals,[1] all communicated in SMART format. Traditionally, organizations have several growth goals and several performance goals.

Growth goals may relate to increasing revenue or profitability, gaining a specific amount of market share in a new industry, or globalization. Performance goals may relate to innovation, technology or supply chain management. These need to be effectively measured with your touchpoints – more so if you have a comprehensive performance management system linking compensation to individual, intervision and corporate goals.

Graphic 10.2: Growth & Performance Goals

Organizational Main Objective	
Growth Goal	**Performance Goal**
Growth Goal	**Performance Goal**
Growth Goal	**Performance Goal**

Other versions of this have been called top-down and bottom-up approaches. The top-down approach is geared for leadership and broad, corporate issues (i.e., growth and performance goals). The bottom-up approach affects people throughout the entire organization (i.e., brand and message strategy).[2] While the growth and performance goals also affect people throughout your organization, even with an engaged strategic planning process, the corporate goals are ultimately determined by leadership. However, the brand and message, if done correctly, affect all touchpoints as they are all potential evangelists, salespeople and recruiters.

Research Targets

As you decide the types of research and research process to use, you must have clear targets to achieve. Do not measure and conduct research without clear targets. While every organization has its own set of targets, we see four general research targets for every organization. These are:

There are two main types of research. The first relates to your brand and message strategy. The second is to measure your growth and performance goals.

1. **Maximize productivity and profitability.** If your research is not providing you with answers to help this, you are missing something.
2. **Generate loyal customers that will stay with you.** Loyal customers tend to be more profitable. These are the right customers.
3. **Have a continuous research process.** All measurement and research should be done on an ongoing basis to constantly track what changes as things do change.
4. **Create an action plan(s).** This is a target many organizations do not consider; however, without this, the first and second targets become very difficult to achieve. This is step 6, discussed in Chapter 11.

As Act is the second A in AL^{2}A and a core differentiator for the AL^{2}A process, it is important to know how AL^{2}A was created. It is based on several other tools, research, best practices and experience. It was initially created for customers, and we quickly learned it could be applied to people as well. There are many other options to measure and conduct research. We will provide a brief analysis of several, including:

- Customer Satisfaction Index (CSI)
- Voice of the Customer (VOC)
- Immersion Experience
- Net Promoter Score (NPS)

CSI

Taken separately, Customer Satisfaction Index (CSI) has been around for a long time and is used by many organizations to measure customer satisfaction. This can take the form of a short or long survey that asks questions after a customer experience. The survey may be on a scale of 1-5, 1-7 or 1-10; using a scale of poor to excellent, not important to very important, dissatisfied to satisfied, etc.

> Creating an action plan is a research objective missed by many organizations, yet it is vital to maximizing productivity and profitability, and generating loyal customers.

CSI questions relate to reactive items such as "Were you satisfied with your experience." Though useful in learning for future improvement, it is a quantitative, reactive process and may occur too late to save the customer. Most importantly, customers are not prioritized and there is no action plan. While this is and can be a useful tool for organizations to gain customers' information and improve, the main issue with CSI is it is reactive – not proactive.[3]

Ultimately, CSI measures customer satisfaction and it has been proven that having satisfied customers is not enough. They must be *completely* satisfied.[4] If this is the case, why only ask about satisfaction?

VOC

Voice of the Customer (VOC) has also been around for a long time. In its simplest form, it is defined as understanding customers' needs. This is done qualitatively by asking open-ended questions. Many equate VOC to customer satisfaction, believing these are synonymous. They are not. VOC focuses on new product development to understand customers' needs for new products.[5]

While some questions are based on a scale similar to CSI, there are also many open-ended, qualitative questions to help get at customers' behaviors and thoughts. It can and should be more proactive than CSI as the purpose is to understand customers' needs to create a new product and/or address these needs; however, its proactive nature is for the entire market – not a specific customer. Based on this, we view this as being <u>reactive</u> – not proactive – as you are still not asking for specific customer needs.[6]

In reflecting on this, our initial effort was to create a new definition for Voice of the Customer that attempted to encompass better prioritization of customers, and a good venue for asking more proactive questions. To do this, we expanded the previous definition of VOC to: a process which identifies, measures, communicates and implements what customers really want. Much more comprehensive as it focuses on measuring, communicating and implementing based on specific customer wants. Despite this, we felt organizations were still using VOC in its traditional sense as customer satisfaction or to only understand needs specific to a new product or service.

> We define VOC as a process which identifies, measures, communicates and implements what customers' really want.

Immersion Experience

Another tool that has been used is an Immersion Experience.[7] This is when members of your organization observe your products and/or services being used by customers. The rationale of simply asking customers is not

> Information gained from traditional VOC may help an entire product or service line, yet it does not address a specific customer's needs.

enough (ala VOC) as they may not provide adequate insight. By observing customers using your products, you are able to see what is working and what isn't. The result is to be proactive and create a new product or service based on these measurement tools.

This typically includes three to four observation sessions involving three to seven key internal touchpoints. Done at multiple locations, the first observation establishes how and what you will be observing, the second presents the product/service to customers so they can become familiar with it, and third creates a question and answer session. A fourth observation may be necessary for an online experience. Once completed, information is compiled with recommendations to improve the product or service.[8]

We like the hands-on method of this tool as it brings organizational leaders and other key stakeholders back to "real life" of the product and/or service. Oftentimes, leaders are far removed from how their products and services truly work and are used. It also provides a venue for the organization to closely interact with customers – sometimes more so than VOC.

Immersion Experience has the highest level of inconsistency as there does not appear to be a consistent process and/or a clear set of questions for customers. This leaves a great deal of freedom to the organization, third party, facilitator, whomever, that is asking the questions and leading the immersion. The result is inconsistency among customers.

While more proactive than CSI, similar to VOC, Immersion Experience's proactive nature is for the entire market – not a specific customer. Based on this, we view this as being reactive – not proactive – as you are still not prioritizing customers and proactively addressing a specific customer's needs.[9]

NPS[10]

Net Promoter Score (NPS) is a newer tool. It was created to be simple and is based on one question, "How likely are you (on a scale of 0 – 10) to recommend (Company X) to a friend or colleague?"

Promoters are those responding with a 9 or 10, and are considered loyal customers willing to tell others about their experience with your organization. Passives respond with a 7 or 8, and are satisfied, yet unenthusiastic and may move to a competitor. Detractors answer 0-6 and are unhappy with the relationship. NPS is the percentage of promoters minus the detractors (those responding with 9 or 10 minus those responding 0 through 6). The belief is NPS provides one of the most reliable indicators of an organization's ability to grow as their research states that Net Promoter leaders have superior growth – averaging more than twice the rate of their competition.

Though it is a relatively easy method, with any tool, it has issues (see Graphic 10.3). Despite the data to support the one question, asking only one question is not enough. More questions are needed, especially proactive ones before the customer experience.[11]

Net Promoter is supposed to be about more than one score. It should include measures linked to growth, focused leadership, methods to ensure adoption organization-wide, synergies with other processes, and infrastructure to support it.[12]

Graphic 10.3 provides a side-by-side comparison of each tool to easily see the positives and issues with each. For example, in

NPS is reactive – not proactive – as it asks about a customer's experience after it has occurred.

Chapter 9, a Fortune 10 firm[13] had been doing NPS for more than 18 months. It was discussed how NPS doesn't provide a method of prioritization as at least one division[14] was conducting NPS with their customers (thousands) for more than nine months before realizing they now had a lot of numbers to identify the promoters, detractors and passives; yet had no clue what to do next.[15] AL²A both addresses what to do next, how to do it, the prioritization of customers, and many other items.

Graphic 10.3: Current Customer Research Options

Research Option	Proactive with Customers	Qualitative or Quantitative	Prioritized Customer Process	Engages Internal Touchpoints	Action Plan for Customer
Customer Satisfaction Index (CSI)	No	Quantitative	No	No	No
Voice of the Customer (VOC)	No (products & services only)	Qualitative	Possibly	No	No (products & services only)
Immersion Experience	No (products & services only)	Qualitative	No	Some	No (products & services only)
Net Promoter Score (NPS)	No	Quantitative	No	No	No

Customers In Action[16]

Toyota and Honda have gained extensive market share at the
expense of GM and Ford. There are many reasons for Toyota and
Honda's market control, and many come down to the partnership
with their suppliers. Toyota and Honda have been proactive with
their suppliers instead of sitting back and waiting for suppliers to be
proactive.

These organizations began by learning about their suppliers'
business – asking questions with a mutual level of respect. As they
typically have no more than three suppliers for each raw material,
they treat all suppliers like Wal-Mart treats it top suppliers. Similar
corporate cultures are also important as this is no different than
hiring a new person. The person may have all the skills in the world,
but if they are not a fit for the culture, they will never succeed.
Culture also relates to brand and message strategy as corporate
culture is similar to your brand personality. Honda and Toyota
expect their suppliers to be brand evangelists.

While suppliers naturally compete with each other on price,
quality, service, etc.; Toyota and Honda conduct innovation sessions
with suppliers to share best practices and knowledge. If each supplier
improves, the result is improvement for Toyota and Honda. They
also constantly measure and conduct research with suppliers by
sending report cards on key performance and growth metrics.

Results from the research are reviewed so lessons can be learned
and shared with suppliers on areas to improve. The research also
provides joint improvement activities whereby Honda, Toyota and
their suppliers partake, providing another venue of information
sharing and continuously learning.

Concluding Thoughts

This chapter presents a means to get to AL^{2}A with Customers while reviewing options for step 5 of the Customer Strategy Process, conducting research. Research with customers is a vital piece of the customer puzzle as it begins to create alignment with your customers. The alignment helps achieve your growth and performance goals, as well as strengthening your brand and message strategy. Through this process, it is believed customers will become evangelists and promoters. The result is a stronger relationship with customers; however, not yet a true partnership. AL^{2}A provides the venue to achieve this.

Chapter 10: Summary

■ There are two main types of customer research. The first relates to your brand and message strategy. The second is to measure your growth and performance goals.

■ There are four general research objectives for every organization.
   1. Maximize productivity and profitability.
   2. Generate loyal customers that will stay with you.
   3. Have a continuous process.
   4. Create an action plan(s).

■ See Graphic 10.3 for a comparison of several current customer research options.

■ What did you learn from the Customers In Action?

Chapter 11

AL²A with Customers

"There are no secrets to success. Don't waste time looking for them. Success is the result of perfection, hard work, learning from failure, loyalty to those for whom you work, and persistence."
– Colin Powell

At this point, we have gone through the first four of six steps of the Customer Strategy Process and you have been presented with four current options to conduct step 5, research. In reflecting on Graphic 10.3, not one of the options presents a venue to complete step 6 – **creating a customer-specific action plan**. AL²A (Ask, Listen, Learn & Act) accomplishes this, as well as providing a better venue for:

- Being proactive with key customers
- Combining both qualitative and quantitative research
- Prioritizing customers
- Involving internal touchpoints

AL²A can also be used for your people to determine emotionally engaged people – complete with action plans. AL²A with Customers is the other bookend.

It incorporates four elements:

- **Ask:** interacting with your customers by proactively asking about their needs.
- **Listen:** understanding what they are asking for and/or need.
- **Learn:** taking this feedback seriously and identifying why gaps may exist.
- **Act:** forming cross-functional intervision teams of touchpoints and creating action plans to address specific customer issues.

Graphic 11.1: AL²A as the Bookends of Strategy

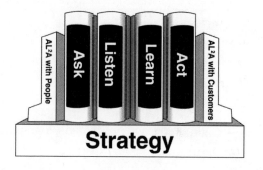

Graphic 11.2 illustrates the six main steps of the AL²A process with Customers. While the AL²A process is a consistent process, these steps are different than AL²A with People as discussed in Chapter 6. When done well, the process is simple. Steps include:

1. Prioritize customers and determine customer-specific teams.
2. Establish attribute criteria.
3. Communicate and implement.
4. Develop and execute action plans.
5. Align the organization.
6. Unite with performance management.

Graphic 11.2: AL²A Process with Customers

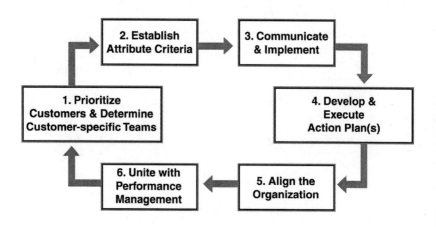

Prioritize Customers and Determine Customer-specific Teams (Step 1)

Prioritization builds off of step 3 of the Customer Strategy Process. Prioritize customers based on revenue (your top 5-10 customers), profitability (your top 5-10), and geographic area and/or industry (another 5-10). Summarized in Graphic 11.3, as a general rule, choose five in each category if you have 100-200 customers and choose up to 10 per category if you have more than 200 customers. Global organizations should do this in each region for a maximum of 40 per global region (North America, Latin America, Asia Pacific and Europe). Small and mid-sized companies with less than 100 customers should focus on a combination of profitability and revenue customers, choosing 5-10 total based on the total number of customers.

> The first step in AL²A with Customers is to prioritize customers and determine customer-specific teams.

Graphic 11.3: Prioritized Customers Based on Total Customers

Total Customers	Revenue	Profitability	Geography/Industry	Prioritized Customers
201 or more (2 + global regions)	10/region	10/region	10 - 20/region	30 - 40/region
201 or more (1 global region)	10	10	10 - 20	30 - 40
100 - 200	5	5	5 - 10	15 - 20
<100	1 - 4	1 - 4	1 - 2	5 - 10

The formation of customer-specific teams is determined once customers have been prioritized. Begin with sales, as this intervision typically is ultimately responsible for the customer partnership. If you have done a quality job prioritizing customers, it should be clear which salesperson is responsible for each prioritized customer. If these are as important customers as they should be, several internal touchpoints from other intervisions should be interacting with them.

For example, in our Wal-Mart example with the food manufacturer, the following intervisions may impact this partnership: sales, marketing, operations, distribution, logistics, transportation, research & development, IT and finance. The customer-specific team may include a person from each of these intervisions, preferably in a leadership or next generation leadership position, each providing a different level of expertise and growth potential. In a large organization, we suggest a minimum of 4 team members (sales plus 3 others) and a maximum of eight, depending on high impact touchpoints and subject to change during the process.

Mid-sized organizations may have a team of 2 to 3 members (including sales), while small organizations may only have 1 to 2 members. There are obvious resource issues to people's time; however, if your people are not investing time with your priority customers, a competitor will.[1] When we discuss step 6 (uniting with performance management), the goals of the team become important as these become individual people performance goals as well.

Once the team is formed, the leader (sales) should schedule the first of several meetings to discuss the entire AL²A process and train members so the team is aware of what will occur and what is expected of them (making this chapter helpful reading).

> Once the customer team is formed, the first meeting should focus on training and educating team members on the AL²A process.

A key discussion item for a second meeting is which customer touchpoints should be involved in AL²A. Just as you have formed a customer-specific intervision team internally, you want to conduct this process for multiple customer touchpoints. This may include the main contact, finance, purchasing, distribution, etc. – similar people to those on your team – as you want feedback across your customer's intervisions (think 360-degree review). This is a very important element where all members of the internal team should have input.

A final recommended item during this step is to engage an external independent group. The group should be completely aligned with each customer-specific team and serve as a guide through this process. At a minimum, this should be done the first time going through AL²A as it will be a new experience for everyone involved. We have also found the external presence to be useful in implementing the process – specifically the qualitative aspect – and will demonstrate this during the Customers In Action in this chapter.

This step should take no more than two weeks to complete and can be completed in as little as one day.

Establish Attribute Criteria (Step 2)

At the second or third meeting, the team should establish attribute criteria for the quantitative part of AL²A. When thinking of attributes, consider items such as words or phrases from your brand and message positioning, topics related to your growth and performance goals, key

> The second step in AL²A with Customers is to establish attribute criteria to create the quantitative and qualitative measurement tool.

organizational metrics (think performance management), and core competencies or deficiencies. These items should then be discussed and prioritized to comprise your quantitative measurement tool.

AL²A with People discussed having specific categories and specific questions. AL²A with Customers is no different as the categories and questions must be customized and personalized for each and every organization as each of their customers is different. This is another key way AL²A is different from other research options as while the process is consistent and standardized, we do not profess to tell any organization what its attributes are.

Here is where a partnership with a third party should help as they can facilitate this discussion from an independent perspective. Categories may relate to corporate culture, sales, service, communication, packaging, etc.

While questions will vary, there are three that should be on every AL²A quantitative measurement tool:[2]

- Will you continue to purchase and grow with Company X?
- Do you recommend Company X to others?
- Are you completely satisfied with Company X?

This quantitative aspect includes other variables. We suggest using a 1-10 scale[3] and having customers rate in three areas:[4]

- Importance: how important is each attribute to the customer
- Performance: how is your organization (Company X) performing in each attribute
- Benchmark: how would the customer rate the benchmark supplier in each attribute

Based on the areas of importance, performance and benchmark, once completed,

> The measurement tool should use a 1-10 scale and incorporate areas related to importance, performance and benchmark, as well as three open-ended questions.

there is a built-in mechanism to create a **Value Index**. This is each performance rating divided by the benchmark rating. Value Index ratings greater than 1.0 indicate your organization is a value leader in the attribute, while ratings of less than 1.0 indicate a gap. This is a quick and easy one-number rating for organizations and leaders to view key measures.

AL²A also incorporates two elements of qualitative research. The first is part of the quantitative measurement tool as there are two open-ended questions:[5]

- What else do you feel is important for Company X to hear for you to be completely satisfied?
- What other products or services would you value from Company X to be completely satisfied?

These questions provide you an opportunity to identify customer needs outside the scope of questions, including "delighters"– items above and beyond what you are currently doing for the customer. Delighters are identified items that are separate from attributes. If applicable, they become part of the action plan and provide an experience of exceeding customers' expectations. Issues related to the attributes are expected to be resolved, while issues and/or items identified from this question should delight the customer and exceed expectations (think innovation).

> Delighters provide customers with an additional level of complete satisfaction as you can truly exceed their expectations with these.

This step should take no more than three weeks to complete and can be completed in as little as two days to have an approved measurement tool.

Communicate and Implement (Step 3)

A completed tool that is not communicated or implemented is a worthless tool. So, how do you effectively communicate and implement AL^{2}A? Communication should occur internally and externally in parallel manner. Internally, appropriate communication vehicles should be used to inform your people about AL^{2}A. Explaining the process and its importance through a series of communications is imperative for employee engagement.

Externally, you have yet to inform your prioritized customers they have been chosen to participate in the AL^{2}A process.[6] Confidentiality in the communication is vital to gain trust from the touchpoints and full disclosure. Touchpoint responses should be averaged to avoid the reporting of individual numbers. This is why a third-party is recommended; to ensure confidentiality, and often, customers are willing to open up more to a third-party. This is unfortunate as you would hope a customer, especially one viewed as a partner would be willing to share their concerns; however, as demonstrated in the Customers in Action this is not always the case.[7]

We found that individual and/or respective customer intervision issues arise and are incorporated into a comprehensive customer action plan. Unfortunately, even though these are prioritized customers, most are very good relationships, but not yet partnerships. An AL²A objective is to strengthen relationships to become partnerships (resulting in maximized profitability, as well as generating loyal customers that will stay with you).

> The third step in AL²A with Customers is to communicate to internal and external touchpoints and implement the process.

Another method to bridge relationships into partnerships through an external partner is to have the partner facilitate the qualitative meeting while having members of your customer-specific team present at the meeting. This takes extensive training with team members as those attending the meeting should be observing. This becomes the L² (Listen and Learn) part of the process as their purpose is not to question or contradict what customers' say. It is to take notes and ask questions to help clarify items, though it may be difficult to hear negative comments about your organization. Customers In Action later in this chapter provides further examples of each situation.[8]

The qualitative meeting brings the quantitative and qualitative together. Another term for the qualitative meeting is a discovery session.[9]

The main purpose is to gather additional information regarding the ratings on the measurement tool, as by itself it only provides numbers. It is difficult to act on numbers alone. And from a positive viewpoint, we have seen extremely positive ratings of 9.0+ which would leave some organizations to believe everything is fine. Yet, occasionally the numbers do not tell the entire story, and the discovery session exposes many issues beneath the ratings to help solidify a partnership and maximize profitability. We have seen attributes scored a 9.0+, only to have the customer reveal they were actually dissatisfied.[10]

Once the discovery session is concluded, you should have all quantitative and qualitative information from multiple customer touchpoints to create your action plan. Timing for this step is largely dependent upon customers' schedules for the discovery session. We have found from the initial customer

> Invite and include all customer touchpoints to the discovery session as an opportunity to learn from each other.

communication through the discovery session should take no more than four weeks and can take as little as one week.

Develop and Execute Action Plan(s) (Step 4)

Developing a customer-specific action plan is another key differentiator and benefit of AL²A. This represents the second "A" in AL²A and includes:

- Scheduling a meeting for the entire customer-specific team
- Reviewing the quantitative and qualitative customer information (provide copies of information in advance so people are prepared)
- Creating the action plan(s)

Trends, issues and opportunities become obvious as you review attribute scores. Compare high importance items with low performance and benchmark items. Pay close attention to the Value Index as this is key indicator of value being offered to the customer.

Trends and key items – often related to low scores – will also arise as you review the comments and information from the qualitative discovery session. As difficult, sometimes lengthy discussions occur, keep in mind the purpose is not to disagree with customer information, rather to incorporate it in the action plan.[11]

> The fourth step in AL^{2}A with Customers is to develop and execute customer-specific action plans. The action plans are a key differentiator of AL^{2}A.

The action plan should be similar to a strategic plan with 3-5 main prioritized goals and 2-4 secondary strategies. You may also want to include positive and negative verbatim comments from customer touchpoints to validate and support the goals.

Initially, this may be a draft action plan.[12] It is important as it provides a venue to communicate with the customer before investing extensive time creating a detailed action plan that will actually be shared with the customer. By doing this, you are telling the customer, "We asked for your feedback, we listened to what you said, we reviewed your information and learned from it, and this is how we are planning to act on it. Did we listen and learn accurately to provide the right actions?"

The customer is able to quickly see the time they and other customer touchpoints invested has been worthwhile. It also allows them to say, "This item really wasn't overly important to us, so it may not need to be included."

Once the draft action plan is approved, the team should meet to create the final action plan.[13] As with a strategic plan, the customer action plan should be in SMART format with clearly defined goals, tactics and deliverables. The purpose of the team is to engage others in the organization, not just the salesperson. Team members should be held accountable for the customer's future satisfaction and this may tie back into the performance management of your organization.

> The action plans should be created similar to your strategic plan. Prioritize items and create in SMART format with clearly defined goals, tactics and deliverables.

As Step 6 of AL²A, uniting with performance management, is still to come, this is where customer goals in the action plan can be aligned with individual goals. This does not mean each team member has an item in the action plan as these are dependent upon the customer. However, if a team member does not have an item, this individual may no longer be needed on the team and it may make sense to add a member from another intervision.

After presenting the plan to the customer, and upon approval, plan execution begins. This includes "working the action plan" and accomplishing the customer's goals. At a minimum, quarterly meetings should be held with the team and customer to review the action plan – no different than a continuous review strategy process.

As with strategy, the customer action plan should be flexible as needs may change during the year. This is why the continuous review is important. We have seen instances where the main customer contact person has changed and the action plan provides a communication opportunity for your organization to engage the new person by reviewing the action plan. The new person may change some items in the plan, and in the process, gain a great deal of respect for your organization being so proactive. This is an opportunity to prove you are proactive when customers' priorities change.

The result of the AL^{2}A process is that each prioritized customer has its own action plan with targeted SMART

> When executing the action plan, follow the continuous review process for your team and with the customer by scheduling quarterly review meetings.

goals aligned with customer-specific team members' individual goals. Again, you initially prioritized these customers for a reason and now you have very specific action plans to proactively grow a partnership and achieve both their goals and your own. Graphic 11.4 appears similar to Graphic 10.3 with a major difference – a new row includes AL^{2}A.

Graphic 11.4: AL^{2}A with Customers vs. Other Options

Research Option	Proactive with Customers	Qualitative or Quantitative	Prioritized Customer Process	Engages Internal Touchpoints	Action Plan for Customer
Ask, Listen, Learn & Act^{SM} (AL^{2}A)	Yes	Qualitative and Quantitative	Yes	Yes	Yes
Customer Satisfaction Index (CSI)	No	Quantitative	No	No	No
Voice of the Customer (VOC)	No (products & services only)	Qualitative	Possibly	No	No (products & services only)
Immersion Experience	No (products & services only)	Qualitative	No	Some	No (products & services only)
Net Promoter Score (NPS)	No	Quantitative	No	No	No

The significant advantages of AL^{2}A include proactivity with customers, being both quantitative and qualitative, having a process to prioritize customers, engaging touchpoints via customer-specific teams, and forming customer-specific action plans.

Timing for this varies as it is based on customer meetings and approvals.[14] The time frame from the beginning of the process through the approval of the action plan can take 8 to 16 weeks depending upon availability and responsiveness of the customer and internal touchpoints. It is well worth it, as now you have action plans for your highest priority customers. The faster the better, as you can begin acting to maximize productivity and profitability.[15]

Align the Organization (Step 5)

In many ways, this step has been occurring throughout the AL^{2}A process. At the beginning, when your organization started the process, leadership should have been communicating its importance to the organization. When the customers were initially prioritized and the customer-specific teams were

> The fifth step in AL^{2}A with Customers is to align the organization. This occurs throughout the entire process – from beginning to end.

formed, more people were getting aligned and engaged. As these team members become more involved, they became emotionally engaged and converted to evangelists to "spread the word" to others. Once full communication began, most people should have heard of AL^{2}A and the communication "connects the dots" for them.

The initial training of customer-specific team members provides them a great deal of knowledge to be "experts" and share this knowledge with others. Team members are typically higher level people and/or top performers, so they are respected by others. Instead of complaining about additional work or another team, people seek to join AL²A teams.

More alignment occurs for those on the customer-team as they are responsible for items in each customer action plan. Those on the team have been chosen as the right people and their performance is tied to this (see Graphic 11.5).

If Suzy is in research & development and on a team with a customer goal to create one new product during the year, Suzy is responsible for this customer goal. This becomes one of Suzy's individual goals. It is already aligned with the customer goal; and Suzy's intervision, research & development, has at least one goal related to creating X number of new products during the year. Suzy is now directly aligned with an intervision goal. Moving up one notch to the organization level, one of the organization's growth goals is to generate $20 million of business from newly created products. Suzy is directly aligned with this organizational goal.

Graphic 11.5: Suzy's Organizational Alignment

| Suzy, R&D | Member of customer-specific team | Customer action plan with goal of creating one new product | R&D intervision with goal of creating X number of new products | Organizational goal to generate $20 million from new products |

Organizations with up to 40 prioritized customers provide ample opportunities for performance management alignment to occur.

You can also average the collective needs of all your prioritized customers to link customer goals. Another method of alignment occurs as several customer action plans are completed. While each customer has its own personalized plan for the customer-specific team to execute, referring back to Graphic 11.2, organizations will be completing 5 to 40+ customer action plans annually. As you begin to review the action plans together, you will see trends among them.

For example, you may see that 80 percent of the customers expect at least one new product created each year, or that 90 percent believe marketing should have more autonomy to make decisions. If this high of a percent of your most prioritized customers are requesting these items, this becomes a great method of helping create your strategic plan as these may become growth and performance items in the strategic plan. Thus, the process becomes complete as not only is the strategy driving AL²A across the organization; the customers are driving goals back to the strategy. People involved with this gain individual goals; linked to customer goals, intervision goals and organization goals. All which leads us to the final step, uniting with performance management.

Unite with Performance Management (Step 6)

Aligning the organization began the linkage with a unified performance management system. To achieve complete success, several factors are necessary:

- Leadership support of AL²A to both People and Customers (see Chapters 6 and 11)
- Strategic organizational foundation (Chapters 1, 2, 3 and 4)
- Communication collaboration – internal and external (Chapters 5, 7, 8, 9 and 10)
- Performance alignment (Chapters 7 and 11)

Graphic 11.6 illustrates the complete linkage. Beginning with the organizational main objective, annual goals are created. These flow to people and customers, becoming both growth and performance goals, as well as those related to your brand and message strategy.

AL²A is the process used to measure the goals and strategy. AL²A is completed for both people and customers to achieve emotional engagement and complete satisfaction. Action plans are completed for people and customers, resulting in individual objectives.

The model works the same if beginning with individual people. Their individual objectives are derived from AL²A with overall people and prioritized customers. This

The sixth step in AL²A with Customers is to unite with performance management. This involves leadership support to people and customers, strategic organizational foundation, communication collaboration and performance alignment.

drives growth and performance goals, as well as brand and message strategy. The results are incorporated into the overall organizational strategy, which drive the main objective.

Graphic 11.6: Uniting with Performance Management

We end this chapter with several Customers In Action for large, mid-sized and small organizations. Each provides rationale and examples of previously stated items. We chose to include these at the chapter's end so you would have a complete understanding of the AL^{2}A process prior to reading these.

Customers In Action (Large organization)

A $3.5 billion global leader in the food and dairy industry had fantastic relationships with its customers. It had been years since it lost a top customer. Unfortunately, leadership was informed of losing its fourth largest customer. The customer had been loyal for more than 15 years.

It was too late to salvage this relationship; however, leadership chose to conduct AL^{2}A with other top customers. One of the organization's core strengths is supply chain management and its distribution channel. The industry average product delivery time is 14 days and this organization can deliver product in 7 days or less. During the process with its third largest customer, they rated supply chain a 4 on importance (on a scale of 10).

As this was a core strength and something the organization prided itself on (and customers paid more for this benefit), this was quite a surprise. The customer commented they never asked for product to be delivered in seven days and 14 days was fine. The salesperson had never asked, listened or learned about this particular topic with the customer. This led to specific action to change the supply chain for this important customer and a stronger relationship striving to become a partnership.

In conducting AL^{2}A with another of its customers, the world's largest retailer, leadership was informed it was the first time a supplier had conducted a proactively, detailed process like this with them. Normally, the retailer does this with suppliers. Both the organization and retailer appreciated third party involvement regarding confidentiality and action plan development. This process thoroughly confirmed the partnership, and revenue and profitability continued to grow at more than 15 percent annually.

To validate including what the customer requests in the action plan, this organization had a customer requesting a new product line. The organization knew it did not have current equipment or skills to create the new products; however, it researched other organizations to form an alliance with, as well as checked into purchasing the equipment and adding staffing. It included these in the action plan – with a hefty price. The customer chose not to proceed with this and was very appreciative of the efforts to listen and act on the request. This strengthened the partnership and generated more business.

Another customer was prioritized based on potential. It was a smaller customer for more than three years with potential to become a top 10 customer. Despite putting one of the best salespeople on the account, business wasn't growing as the customer was loyal to its main supplier. The organization partnered with a third party. The customer-specific team joined for the AL^{2}A discovery session. During the discussion, the customer touchpoints were asked point-blank what the organization needed to do to get business from the main supplier. This generated a discussion of three main items.

They were then asked if the organization did these three items if they would guarantee moving business. They said "no," however, if the organization achieved these three items and sustained them for four months, and then exceeded them for another three months, they would move the business. They stated it didn't make sense to move the business if the organization can only equal what the competitor is doing. Upon leaving the meeting, the salesperson was ecstatic, proclaiming he had been asking that question for three years and did not receive an answer. He was glad they felt comfortable with an independent third party. The result: the organization was able to accomplish and sustain the items, although they did not exceed them. Despite this, while the customer did not move all of the business, they appreciated the willingness to try during the action plan and moved some business with a commitment to future growth.

Customers In Action (Mid-sized organization)

A $200 million global manufacturer of consumer products in the transportation industry conducted AL^{2}A with its prioritized customers. They chose to use a third party partner and not attend the discovery sessions. During the process, two of the top 10 customers informed the partner they were planning to cease doing business with the organization. As confidentiality is vital, the partner asked both customers permission to share this with the president of the organization. Both said yes with a caution that it probably would not make a difference.

Upon informing the president, he contacted both customers, flew to their headquarters and talked through issues. Both relationships have been salvaged and they are working toward a partnership.

A $50 million design build contracting firm performed AL^{2}A with its customers. Business had been growing and the president wanted to know why. In a very competitive industry, why were customers choosing to do business with this organization instead of the competitors? They also chose an external partner and created specific action plans that have not only led to new business opportunities, but stronger partnerships and leadership as well.

The stronger partnerships resulted from their customers' appreciating an organization willing to invest in this process and provide a specific action plan for joint growth. The leadership was

strengthened based on repetitive customer feedback to see and speak
with the president more often as the individual seems "out of
pocket." People within the organization had been requesting this for
years; however, the president felt he didn't need to do it because
business was growing and he trusted his team. Upon hearing this
consistent message with prioritized customers, he has made this part
of his individual goals.

Customers In Action (Small organization)

A $3 million creative marketing organization wanted to grow
business with its prioritized customers. Revenues were good and
steadily growing; however, they realized they were being more
reactive and waiting for customers to contact them with projects
instead of truly having partnerships.

Partnering with an external group and not participating in the
discovery sessions, they discovered a positive and negative
experience. On the positive side, an action plan was created with one
customer that was closely linked with their marketing plan. This
included several new product launches, trade shows and other
marketing materials. While this organization would have received
some of this new business, the customer was planning to distribute it
to others as well. Based on the AL^{2}A process, they agreed to provide
all to the organization because they respected the process and wanted
to grow the relationship into a partnership.

On the negative side, another customer informed the external
group they were going to move to another firm. Respecting the
confidentiality, the partner asked permission to share this with the
president of the organization. Unfortunately, the response was "no"
so the partner did not share this information. During the draft action
plan, the partner shared the ratings and feedback, which were

obviously low and negative. When asked if they would lose the account, respecting confidentiality, the partner replied an inability to respond to the question and recommend contacting the customer to talk directly with them. While this occurred, the relationship was not salvageable; however, the organization learned from this and has incorporated many processes into its organization to prevent this from occurring in the future.

A less than $1 million service organization conducted AL²A with its customers. The president did not want to use an external partner as he felt he had very good partnerships with customers. He performed the process with internal customer-specific teams and received good information – ratings of 9.0+ and very positive feedback. Customer action plans were created, yet business wasn't growing. He then chose an external partner who discovered different information. It appeared customers were not as open and honest as thought, so they were not sharing opportunities for improvement. Upon receiving this new information and revising the action plans, business has been increasing.

Concluding Thoughts

This concludes all pieces of the Strategy, People, Customers puzzle. You are now armed with the entire puzzle. Keep in mind that once the puzzle is complete, it can easily come apart. You must continuously work on your puzzle and search for ways to constantly improve it. This makes it more and more difficult to break apart.

We have provided many examples of real life applications throughout the book with Strategy In Action, People In Action and Customers In Action. The Epilogue provides a high-level view of an acquisition and integration as this presents a great example of applying Strategy, People and Customers to summarize the puzzle.

Chapter 11: Summary

■ AL²A with customers consists of six steps.
1. Prioritize customers and determine customer-specific teams.
2. Establish attribute criteria.
3. Communicate and implement.
4. Develop and execute action plans.
5. Align the organization.
6. Unite with performance management.

■ Prioritize customers and determine customer-specific teams consists of:
- Determining the customers to prioritize. The total number is based on your total number of customers.
- Choosing multiple customer touchpoints within each prioritized customer.
- Creating customer-specific teams of 4-8 people for large organizations and 1-2 people for small organizations.
- Deciding if you will engage an external partner.
- Time ranges from one day to two weeks.

■ Establish attribute criterion consists of:
- Creating the measurement tool based brand and message positioning, and other key performance indicators.
- Personalizing the categories and questions as every customer and its touchpoints are different.
- Focusing on importance, performance and benchmark indicators.
- Including three open-ended questions to have a qualitative component.
- Time ranges from two days to three weeks.

- Communicate and implement consists of:
  - Communicating internally and externally.
  - Calling prioritized customers to introduce them to the process, e-mailing information to all customer touchpoints, and scheduling the discovery session.
  - Ensuring confidentiality if needed by partnering with an external firm.
  - Time ranges from one week to four weeks.

- Develop and execute action plan(s) consists of:
  - Reviewing qualitative and quantitative information, as well as the Value Index.
  - Prioritizing items similar to the strategic planning process.
  - Creating a draft action plan and having customer validation.
  - Developing a customer-specific action plan in SMART format.
  - Executing the plan using a continuous review method.
  - Time is one year as the process should be done annually, with continuous review meetings scheduled quarterly with the customer-specific team and the customer.

- Align the organization consists of:
  - Educating, communicating and training people throughout the entire process – from beginning to end as this is a continuous step.
  - Creating evangelists and promoters from your people, customer-specific teams and customers.
  - Aligning the customer-specific action plans with your strategy and strategic plan.

- Unite with performance management consists of:
  - Focusing on leadership support to people and customers.
  - Having a strong strategic organizational foundation.
  - Concentrating on communication collaboration.
  - Engaging in performance alignment.
  - See Graphic 11.6.

- What did you learn from the Customers In Action?

Epilogue

Solving the Profit Puzzle

*"What is success? I think it is a mixture
of having a flair for the thing that you are doing;
knowing that it is not enough, that you have got to have
hard work and a certain sense of purpose."
– Margaret Thatcher*

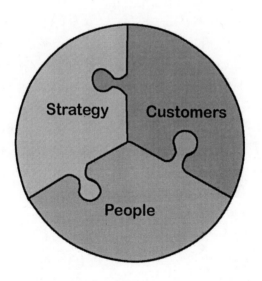

Sections I, II and III have focused on Strategy, People and Customer respectively. Throughout, we have demonstrated how these three puzzle pieces fit together for organizations to achieve greater profitability and success. As with any puzzle, there is not a specific beginning and end point. So, does an organization begin with strategy, people or customers as the first piece? The response depends where your organization is in its particular life cycle.

One method is to begin with your strategy, determine your people elements through AL^2A with People and other items described in Section II, and then focus on your customer strategy. Another approach reveals how your people strategy can be defined through AL^2A with People, which flows to your strategy and outward toward your customers via AL^2A with Customers. A third way is to focus on your customer strategy with AL^2A with Customers, and align this with your people strategy through performance management as part of your overall strategy.

We provide another view of how the puzzle creates greater success. The concept of Strategy, People and Customers may seem challenging, and it is. Profitability and success are not easy. Completing the puzzle and executing it effectively throughout an entire organization can be difficult. Completing the puzzle requires assistance from all internal and external touchpoints. While there are other processes interacting with all internal and external touchpoints, we believe an acquisition and integration presents an example of how the puzzle can be completed as it is an organizational end-to-end process needing strategy, people and customers to succeed.

Acquisitions & Integrations

While acquisitions and integrations are a complex process and could encompass its own book, we have tried to simplify it to a high-level capstone. We begin early in the acquisition process as the strategy is being formulated, and take you through the involvement of people and customers to achieve success.

We use this as an example because 2006 was a record year for acquisition deal activity at $3.7 trillion globally,[1] and despite this, up to 75 percent of acquisitions fail to achieve their financial objectives.[2] This is a process in dire need of increased success and the complete puzzle of Strategy, People and Customers.

There are many steps and components of an acquisition and integration process. To somewhat simplify the process, we begin with a letter of intent being signed and the due diligence process about to commence.[3] One issue related to acquisitions and integrations is the creation of a strategy throughout the process. At its highest level, many organizations have an acquisition goal, which may read, "We will actively look to acquire companies to grow market share." The strategy is to acquire companies, while the execution is to integrate these. A gap is that each step of this process requires its own unique strategy and implementation.

Several acquisition and integration process steps will be reviewed, demonstrating how each needs strategy, people and customers to succeed.[4] The goal is to use an acquisition and integration as a comprehensive example summarizing the three puzzle pieces.

Due Diligence

Once a letter of intent is signed, due diligence must be viewed as both a process and strategy. Most organizations have detailed due diligence checklists and questions to ask; however, much of this information relates only to financials. While the financial information is a core element to the acquisition, we have discovered the inclusion of people and customers to be as vital.

The first step includes forming a due diligence team. The team should include a leader – possibly someone from finance or business development – and absolutely include the integration leader[5] and representatives from core intervisions. By forming the team, we have already included people into our puzzle. There should be a clear process for people selected for the team. It may be top performers or specific roles. While it is good to have consistency of team members, there is also opportunity to use this as part of your performance management system for key people whereby team participation may be part of an individual's annual performance goals.

The due diligence team leader should present the strategy to team members. This may take many forms, including a review of onsite rules, [6] questions to ask, what to look for, and what synergies and/or expenses should be known. People from the target company become involved during the process as each intervision may speak with either a senior leader of the target company or an intervision leader.

Customers enter into the due diligence process as the diligence team should gather information about key customers. Gaining these customers can be a key to the deal. We have experienced organizations that lose up to 30 percent or more of newly acquired customers after an acquisition because their due diligence strategy was not thorough enough to capture key information.

Integration Strategy

Integration strategy is another core process within an acquisition and integration strategy. This should begin as early as the deal allows it, which should be well before the deal closes. An error some organizations make is to wait until the deal closes and then begin integration. This is too late.[7] Beginning as early as the deal allows takes many forms and will be different for each organization. In our experiences, a best practice is to begin at least 45 days before the deal is scheduled to close.

To build an effective integration strategy, you need a team of people. The team may include some due diligence team members or all new members. It should consist of the integration leader, who is ultimately responsible for the success of the integration, as well as representation from key intervisions from both your organization and the newly acquired company. Embracing members from the newly acquired company is important as they are the experts in their business and it begins to form alignment and engagement among the two organizations.

The strategy is formed from information gathered during due diligence related to the synergies and issues. An online technology-based integration system is one of the best venues as it provides all team members and key stakeholders with an ability to easily view the entire strategy via an online format. This includes a similar dashboard of measures as previously described in Chapter 7, relating to integration synergies and measurements, as well as step-by-step activity lists for each intervision and person. The activity lists should have co-dependencies so everyone knows when an activity is due and what happens to the timeline if something is not accomplished. In effect, this online technology-based format creates its own integration synergy and alignment, for all touchpoints helping with profitability and success.

Thus far, integration strategy has included two of our three puzzle pieces – strategy and people. A more detailed people strategy for newly acquired people will soon be discussed. Your integration strategy should also include other components such as IT, Operations, etc. and the technology-based system introduced earlier will assist with these.[8] As our puzzle is focused on customers and people, we have chosen to focus on these.

As for customers, they are a core part of the strategy for reasons previously discussed in the due diligence section and become part of the integration strategy. Your integration strategy should include a customer strategy. The customer strategy should begin with a comprehensive review of all new customers. Think back to the 4 R's and determining if they are the right customers.[9] Another best practice is to place customers in A – D Tiers, similar with the people discussion in Chapter 5. Tier A customers should have been established during due diligence, with Tiers B – D becoming part of the integration strategy.

As with people, begin the customer integration with Tier A customers and so on. You may conduct all six steps of the Customer Strategy Process discussed in Chapter 9 or choose to focus on AL^2A with Tier A customers. The AL^2A process is recommended with Tier A customers as it creates a venue to interact with these customers through an Ask, Listen, Learn and Act process. The deliverable of a customer-specific action plan creates closer relationship with these customers – working toward a partnership – and an accelerated pace of profitability as you become aligned with customers much faster.[10]

Cultural Assessment and Communication

While people are part of the integration strategy, we chose to view them as a separate section related to cultural assessment and communication. Cultural assessment during an acquisition and integration is often over-looked, and in our experiences is one of the major reasons integrations do not meet financial objectives.

During due diligence, there is extensive focus on financial information and little focus on people and organizational culture.

Because of this, newly acquired top performers may leave the company, or the two cultures do not mix, leading to low morale and decreases in product quality and customer service, resulting in lost business. The result has a direct correlation with the overall integration financial objectives as these items are typically not taken into consideration during the process.

This can be averted with a cultural assessment during due diligence and a people strategy created in the integration strategy. Think back to our discussion in Section I relating to the formation of the main objective and corresponding values. The cultural assessment should provide a rating scale of these types of items when speaking with leaders at the target company. Leaders exhibit much of the corporate culture, so they should exemplify the culture to help you determine if there is a fit with your organization. In some instances, this may be enough to stop the acquisition process, regardless of the financials, as it may be too difficult to effectively integrate the two organizations. The key is to recognize and assess this prior to the deal closing.

Understanding culture prior to the deal close allows it to be included in the integration strategy and synergies. Go through a detailed analysis of roles and people at the newly acquired location, creating a plan for interacting with them. Prioritize top performers as they are the most likely to leave, and if so, may provide a short- to medium-term negative impact on the synergies and profitability.

Within the first 60 days, conduct AL^2A with People to determine baseline measures of emotional engagement. An important aspect of the success of AL^2A is communication. This presents a transition to communication related to acquisitions and integrations.

An all-inclusive communication plan is a must for the integration strategy. As with other unsuccessful integrations we have explained, a lack of communication plan and tactics were common denominators. Creating a communication plan prior to the deal close and including it in the integration strategy provides all touchpoints with an understanding of what will be communicated, how, when, where and why.

Your strategy should be reproduced in the communication plan. This includes your main objective, goals and strategies. Newly acquired people must understand these items to begin to create emotional engagement so they can become evangelists and salespeople. They must identify with and appreciate your corporate culture to determine if they want to be part of it.

This is not just communication to newly acquired people on the day the deal closes. This is communication occurring throughout the entire integration to people, customers and suppliers – all touchpoints. The integration leader is typically the "voice" of this communication as the main contact point, and intervision leaders from both organizations must understand the plan and their roles in it. As the people strategy is implemented via roles and people identification, the communication plan should address this. And, as AL^2A occurs, communication should transpire throughout this process – including the Act, as items from the results need to be incorporated into the communication plan.[11]

As cultural assessment and the communication plan are completed prior to the deal close and are part of the integration strategy, you have noted that a great deal of the people strategy is implemented once the deal is actually closed. This brings us to the next step of integration implementation.

Integration Implementation

We have noted how components of integration strategy, people strategy, customer strategy, cultural assessment and communication occur prior to the close of deal, in addition to after it. The implementation of an acquisition and integration could be its own book. A leap of faith must be taken to achieve success during an acquisition and integration. As with your organization, follow the three puzzle pieces of Strategy, People and Customers; and you will achieve greater success by maximizing productivity and profitability. The same is for an integration implementation.

We have demonstrated that there is a strategy for the entire acquisition and sub-strategies for target selection, due diligence, integration, people and customers. As we focus on people, its strategy flows back to the previously mentioned steps of the acquisition process, as well as processes from Section II. The same is for customers and the relation to Section III. From this, we have demonstrated how Strategy, People and Customers help both organizations and integrations. The same puzzle pieces are needed and must be executed to perfection.

Lessons Learned

A final step to both the acquisition and integration process, and the Strategy, People, Customers model associated with your organization is to continuously learn and improve on everything. It was mentioned that the puzzle pieces must be executed to perfection. We recognize that perfection is not possible. However, we have found organizations, people and processes that strive for perfection know when to take one step back to take two steps forward. It is important to play to win instead of playing not to lose.

You must take the time throughout each and every process and puzzle to see what worked and what didn't. These lessons learned apply to continuous learning, helping achieve greater success. We wish you good luck and continued success as you solve your puzzle!

Appendix A: Puzzle Processes

*"I always remember an epitaph... it says,
'Here lies Jack Williams. He done his damnedest.'
I think that is the greatest epitaph a man can have
– when he gives everything that is in him to do the job
he has before him. That is all you can ask of him."*
– Harry S. Truman

In our quest to answer the question of **"How can organizations become more profitable and successful?"** we have focused on Strategy, People and Customers.

Each puzzle piece is comprised of a process or set of steps. To help avoid potential confusion and err on the side of clarity, we have listed the main processes and/or steps. There is direct correlation with Sections, Chapters, chapter summaries and graphics; and this provides these items in one Appendix for those preferring simplicity.

Section I: Strategy

Strategy
- Align intervisions
- Determine present situation
- Create a main objective (include the five characteristics)
- Develop goals for the organization and each intervision
- Construct strategies for the goals
- Generate SMART tactics to execute the goals
- Conduct a continuous review process

Innovation
- There are 6 types of innovation (Chapter 4)
- There are several paths to achieve innovation (Graphic 4.1)
- Hold an innovation session (Graphic 4.2)

Section II: People

People
- Focus on the 4 R's (Recruit, Retrain, Reward, Retention)
- Introduce the fifth R as the first R (Roles)
- Determine if you have the right roles related to strategic effort and performance variability (Graphic 5.1)
- Once A – D roles are determined, clarify if you have the right people in these roles related to culture and performance (Graphic 5.2)

AL^{2}A with People
- Ask, Listen, Learn & Act (Graphic 6.2)
- Employ the 4 C's (Confidentiality, Communication, Concise, Customized)
- Use a SMART format
- Achieve emotional engagement

Performance Management
- Emotionally engaged people help align intervisions, creating successful organizations
- Organizations view performance management beginning with structure, placement, performance, development and reward (Graphic 7.1)
- People view performance management beginning with reward, development, performance, placement and structure (Graphic 7.1)
- Performance management begins with your strategy/strategic plan and flows to your intervision goals to people goals. Measurement and communication occur throughout the process.

- View the performance management system via Graphic 7.2
- A dashboard with a red, yellow and green light structure provides the organization and people with a quick view of success of the goals (Graphic 7.3)

Section III: Customers

Customers

- Focus on the 4 R's (Recruit, Retrain, Reward, Retention) plus the fifth R (Roles)
- Concentrate on demographics and psychographics
- Create your own version of WIRED (Wisdom, Improve Capabilities, Results, Eager to Learn, Desire to Commit)

Customer Strategy Process (Graphic 9.1)

- Step 1: Assess the current situation
- Step 2: Determine internal touchpoints
- Step 3: Prioritize customers
- Step 4: Evaluate research needs, objectives and budgets
- Step 5: Conduct research
- Step 6: Develop action plan(s)

Step 5: Conduct Research

- This step is a core element of getting to AL^2A (Chapter 10)
- This relates to Growth Goals and Performance Goals

AL^2A with Customers

- Ask, Listen, Learn & Act. The Act part relates to Step 6 of the Customer Strategy Process (develop action plans).
- AL^2A is a process that can be completed for both people (internally) and customers/suppliers (externally)

- The AL^{2}A with Customers process consists of 6 steps (Graphic 11.2):
  - Step 1: Prioritize customers and determine customer-specific teams
  - Step 2: Establish attribute criteria
  - Step 3: Communicate and implement
  - Step 4: Develop and execute action plan(s)
  - Step 5: Align the organization
  - Step 6: Unite with performance management
- Step 1 of AL^{2}A is a deeper dive of Step 3 of the Customer Strategy Process as it prioritizes your most important customers vs. all customers
- Step 4 of AL^{2}A is the implementation of Step 6 of the Customer Strategy Process as both relate to developing action plans
- Step 6 of AL^{2}A brings together the AL^{2}A with People process and performance management so performance management effectively measures both growth and performance goals related to both people and customers (Graphic 11.6)
- Key differentiators for AL^{2}A compared to other currently used customer research methods includes:
  - Proactive with customers vs. reactive
  - Both qualitative and quantitative vs. one or the other
  - Prioritizes customers vs. guessing
  - Customer-specific teams that engage internal touchpoints vs. a sales-only initiative
  - Customer-specific action plans vs. no action plan or a broad-based plan for a specific product/service

Epilogue

Solving the Profit Puzzle

- Each step in an acquisition and integration includes Strategy, People and Customers. Considering all information from Sections I, II and III, a successful integration needs all three puzzle pieces.
- Strive for perfection. Continuously improve through lessons learned to achieve greater success as you solve your puzzle.

Appendix B: About the Research

This book has focused extensively on interactions and observations with hundreds of organizations and thousands of professionals across many industries. For more than 15 years these interactions and observations have occurred causing reflection on one question: **How can organizations become more profitable and successful?**

The Strategy, People, Customers puzzle was created to answer this question. It resulted from countless discussions with organizational leaders. AL^2A resulted from other best practices, discussions, experiences and trial-and-error; and has been completed with several organizations to date. As we respect the confidentiality of all organizations, other than general references to Wal-Mart, Toyota and Honda; no specific organizations are mentioned.

Based on all of this, we feel it necessary to provide some background about the author, David Yeghiaian, as a majority of the research is based on his personal interactions, observations and discussions. This includes:

- Two instances of involvement with state government and one with federal government. Working for a U.S. Congressman and State Senator, as well as the Wisconsin Department of Transportation. State and federal government is an industry to its own.

- Interacting with organizations with 100 or more people across a six county region occurred while at the Wisconsin Department of Transportation. This included training leaders from these organizations – more than 20 leaders per day for 20 different days – 400+ interactions.

- Doing sales for a small business provided another opportunity to speak with leaders of other small and mid-sized organizations.

- Working for a non-profit sports organization that had more than 4 million members nationwide – not to mention global alliances. The members participated in the sport for fun, and many were business leaders in their own right.

- Playing a lead role in branding and marketing efforts for a Fortune 200 global organization. Interacting with leaders in a large breadth of industries across the world, as well as visiting and benchmarking with a global firm that had one of the top five market capitalizations in the world; and another, a telecommunications provider, that was one of the fastest growing brands of all time.

- Participating in the spin-off of a $70 million dot com company, including its business and marketing strategy.

- Leading an extremely experienced team at a $200 million firm as the average experience of the 13 member team was more than 25 years. Conducting research and change management on a global scale that included achieving 99 percent brand recognition.

- Working for a more than $3 billion global food and dairy firm that is one of the best kept secrets in the world. Assisting with acquisitions and integrations, and interacting with a "who's who" list of customers and leaders – including the number one retailer in the world.

- Partnering with a Fortune 150 organization as it continues to expand and having discussions with key leaders in its nationwide distribution network.

- Speaking with a division of a Fortune 10 organization about improving its processes and customer relationships.

- Owning a business, which has allowed networking, discussing, engaging and learning from hundreds of small, medium and large organizations.
- Teaching at universities as an adjunct instructor and engaging students – many returning adults in leadership roles – in discussions about Strategy, People and Customers.
- Asking more than 150 students whether people (defined as employees) or customers are more important to an organization. Almost 58 percent chose customers, while 43 percent chose people. There is not necessarily a right or wrong response to this question; however, the responses validate both are needed – along with strategy – to achieve success.
- Volunteering on boards and other community activities, providing another venue to Ask, Listen, Learn and Act with business leaders.

In the end, the research was conducted using a form of AL^2A. It was continually Asking, Listening and Learning from anyone and everyone. The result was Acting. Acting to create the Strategy, People, Customers puzzle as a model to achieve organizational success; and the AL^2A process with People and Customers.

If you feel your organization has achieved success through Strategy, People and Customers; and/or has successfully implemented AL^2A, please contact us so we can share it in a future book, on our website and via presentations.

Notes

Introduction

[1] Jennings, Jason (2002). *Less is More*. New York: The Penguin Group.

[2] Collins, Jim (2001). *Good to Great*. New York: Harper Business.

[3] Mankins, Michael C. & Steele, Richard. "Stop Making Plans, Start Making Decisions." Harvard Business Review. January 2006: 76-84.

[4] Fleming, John, H., Coffman, Curt, & Harter, James K. "Manage Your Human Sigma." Harvard Business Review. July-August 2005: 107-114.

[5] This is a new process created by David Yeghiaian. A service mark for this exclusive process has been created.

[6] Fleming, John, H., Coffman, Curt, & Harter, James K. "Manage Your Human Sigma." Harvard Business Review. July-August 2005: 107-114.

[7] McConnell, Beth. "Employee Loyalty, Engagement Grow Same Qualities in Customers." Society for Human Resource Management. September 2005. < http://www.shrm.org/hrnews _published/archives/CMS_014189.asp> (Accessed May 2006).

Section I

[1] Jennings, Jason (2002). *Less is More*. New York: The Penguin Group.

Chapter 1

[1] Choi, Thomas Y. & Liker, Jeffrey K. "Building Deep Supplier Relationships." Harvard Business Review. December 2004: 104-113.

Chapter 2

[1] Mankins, Michael C. & Steele, Richard. "Stop Making Plans, Start Making Decisions." Harvard Business Review. January 2006: 76-84.

[2] Ibid.

[3] Ibid.

[4] Organizational goals are not in SMART format as they are more broad-based and may extend over a 3-year period. They represent what your organization is striving to achieve and each year, both intervision goals and strategies are in SMART format to achieve the organizational goals.

Chapter 4

[1] At the time of this writing, Leonardo Da Vinci was extremely popular based on the movie and book, "The Da Vinci Code." Brown, Dan (2003). *The Da Vinci Code*. New York: Doubleday.

[2] When we started this book, the intent was to include a discussion on innovation in Chapter 3. However, based on continued research and discussions with business leaders, we dedicated Chapter 4 to innovation. Our belief is that innovation is a facet of strategy, yet its importance has earned the topic its own chapter.

[3] Conlin, Michelle. "Champions of Innovation." BusinessWeek: Inside Innovation. June 2006: 18-26.

[4] Franzke, Brandon. "Fuel Injection." Illumin. Volume 2: Issue iii. March 1, 2002. University of Southern California Viterbi School of Engineering. <http://illumin.usc.edu> (Accessed March 2007).

[5] Garsten, Ed. "Cadillac Spins New Sales With Branded Bicycles." The Detroit News. July 2006. <http://www.detnews.com/2005/autosinsider/0507/26/C01-258961.htm> (Accessed February 2007).

[6] Kelley, Thomas. "The Ten Faces of Innovation." Manufacturing Matters! Conference. Midwest Airlines Center, Milwaukee, May 15, 2006.

Section II

[1] Grensin-Pophal, Linda. "Follow Me." HR Magazine. February 2000: Vol. 45, No. 2: 36-41.

Chapter 5

[1] Bliss, William. G. "Cost of Employee Turnover." The Advisor. 2006. <http://www.isquare.com/turnover.cfm> (Accessed July 2006).

[2] Buckingham, Marcus & Clifton, Donald O. (2001). *Now, Discover Your Strengths*. New York: The Free Press.

[3] Huselid, Mark A., Beatty, Richard W. & Becker, Brian E. "A Players or Positions?" Harvard Business Review. December 2005: 110-117.

[4] Ohno, Taiichi (1988). *Toyota Production Systems – Beyond Large-Scale Production*. New York: Productivity Press.

Chapter 6

[1] AL^2A with Customers is discussed in greater detail in Section III.

[2] Fleming, John, H., Coffman, Curt, & Harter, James K. "Manage Your Human Sigma." Harvard Business Review. July-August 2005: 107-114.

[3] Ibid.

[4] Ibid.

[5] Cook, Kevin. "The Greatest Show in Sports: SportsCenter." Playboy: January 2007: 60.

[6] Thackray, John. "Feedback for Real." Gallup Management Journal. March 2001: <http://gmj.gallup.com/content/default.aspx?ci=811> (Accessed July 2006).

[7] If conducted electronically (our preferred method), a third party can also insure confidentiality by programming the system so each person receives a "coded" link so only this person can participate, which further helps with confidentiality.

[8] The first communication should occur approximately 30 days prior to launch of AL^2A and the second about 2 weeks prior. If a third is done, do it 1 week prior. This results in increased response rates from your people.

[9] Our process is approximately 60-75 total questions, taking roughly 15 minutes. Most questions are based on a 1-7 or 1-10 scale, ranging from Completely Disagree (1) to Completely Agree (7 or 10, depending upon the scale), making it easy for people to click a number. There are also up to three open-ended questions and some qualifier questions relating to location, intervision, etc.

[10] Thackray, John. "Feedback for Real." Gallup Management Journal. March 2001: <http://gmj.gallup.com/content/default.aspx?ci=811> (Accessed July 2006). Based on our research and experience, we have never used all 12 questions. The main question neither used nor preferred by organizations, is "Do you have a best friend at work?" While we understand the importance of this question related to engagement, we created a different question. Many

categories also have consistency by containing specific best practice questions, such as; (a) I am confident in the leadership of Company X; (b) Company X cares about its people; (c) Company X seeks to provide win-win outcomes; and (d) Company X clearly communicates to all people.

[11] Reichheld, Fred (2006). *The Ultimate Question*. Boston: Harvard Business School Publishing.

[12] Based on our research, we have found the 1-7 scale works best when using AL^2A with People (employees) as our observation is that it provides easier understanding and communication. With customers, a 1-10 scale is becoming increasingly popular, based largely on Net Promoter Score, which will be discussed in more detail in Section III. As we strongly believe in consistency, with more research, it is believed a 1-10 scale ultimately will prove to be better for people – and achieve consistency.

[13] Use your preferred Internet search engine and type in "360 review" and you'll see many descriptions.

[14] Individually, the costs – time and money – add up for an organization to implement these methods. Sometimes, it is more practical to outsource the data gathering and analysis of these processes to third-party advisors. As they specialize in these processes, their efficiencies contribute to your cost-savings – not to mention confidentiality of information. AL^2A should always offer up to three open-ended questions for your people to add other information you may not have asked. These three are most effective: (a) What are the most important things for Company X to improve upon to become more productive and successful? (b) What can Company X do to make you emotionally engaged (or remain emotionally engaged)? and (c) Please include any other comments. These questions provide differentiation for AL^2A as people are able to provide quantitative and qualitative feedback. The result is a more comprehensive process for collecting feedback, helping with Listen, Learn and Act.

[15] Intervisions is a new term created and mentioned in Chapter 1. It relates to departments, divisions, business units, functional areas, etc. and aligning these together to cohesively share the same vision (visions together).

[16] SMART was discussed in Chapter 2. In addition, use your preferred Internet search engine and type in "SMART goals" and you'll see many other descriptions.

[17] The Act process should be familiar as it was discussed in Section I. As you should do with your strategy, the same should be done with AL^2A. This is what makes AL^2A unique. While Strategy, People and Customers represent a puzzle, each piece of the puzzle is completed with an AL^2A puzzle of its own.

Chapter 7

[1] Grensing-Pophal, Lin. "Follow Me." HR Magazine. February 2000: Vol. 45, No. 2: 36-41.

[2] Lockwood, Nancy R. "Leveraging Employee Engagement for Competitive Advantage: HR's Strategic Role." 2007 SHRM Research Quarterly.

[3] Finigan, Kathleen. "Setting Specific Goals Improves an Employee's Performance." The Business Review. June 1998. <http://albany.bizjournals.com/albany/stories/1998/06/08/smallb3. html?page=2> (Accessed February 2007).

[4] Through our research and performing AL^2A, we have analyzed this with thousands of people from many organizations, and rarely do we see compensation as the primary motivator. Rather, items such as recognition, training, career advancement and learning rank higher.

[5] I would like to thank Claudio Diaz for his prior insights, thoughts and discussion on this topic, as well as a structure for this graphic.

[6] Daniel, Teresa A., J.D. & Metcalf, Gary S., PhD. "The Fundamentals of Employee Recognition." May 2005. Society of Human Resources Management: White Paper.

[7] There are many different methods for a bonus structure such as this. Many may not provide people with a percent of the bonus if the overall company goal of revenues/profitability is not met (e.g., this goal has a 0 percent multiplier, so it may cancel all other goals if not met). While we understand the rationale of this, we believe it is counter to performance management and attaining emotionally engaged people. It can be de-motivating to people that have achieved their individual goals and/or their intervision goals, yet receive a 0 percent bonus. A true performance management is reliant on each component (individual, intervision, organization), yet is designed to reward each as a step in the process.

Chapter 8

[1] Fishman, Charles. "Wal-Mart You Don't Know." Fast Company December 2003. <www.fastcompany.com> (Accessed August 2006).

[2] Customers asking suppliers to reduce their cost is common in virtually every industry we are aware of. This is not a Wal-Mart only phenomenon. The key for suppliers is to learn how to reduce costs to their customers, while maintaining and/or maximizing their profitability.

[3] Williams, David H. "The Strategic Implications of Wal-Mart's RFID Mandate." Directions Magazine. July 29, 2004. <http://www.directionsmag.com/article.php?article_id=629&trv=1>. (Accessed August 2006). RFID is an automatic identification method, relying on storing and remotely retrieving data using devices called RFID tags or transponders. The tags are a successor to the Universal Product Code label, enabling entire pallets of goods to be counted and tracked with a single tag that is scanned by a laser. This is different from the UPC, which required the scanning of individual items.

4 Fishman, Charles. "Wal-Mart You Don't Know." <u>Fast Company</u>
   December 2003. <<u>www.fastcompany.com</u>> (Accessed August
   2006). Our mention of pickles may be an odd example in a
   discussion of Wal-Mart's control of RFID implementation with its
   suppliers. However, it is a major pickle supplier – Vlasic – that is a
   notable victim in Wal-Mart's influence over its suppliers.
   Apart from the RFID demands, Wal-Mart drastically drove down
   the price of one of Vlasic's niche products, its one gallon container
   of kosher dills. Wal-Mart priced the pickles for less than $3, and
   while Vlasic had the same costs, its margins were reduced to next
   to nothing because of the low price they were pressured to
   maintain.

5 Quality isn't mentioned because this is an expectation of Wal-Mart
   and other customers regarding products and services.

6 To some, this may sound like a lot of Wal-Mart bashing, while to
   others, it may just sound like good business. Considering Wal-
   Mart's tremendous success and its somewhat suspicious
   reputation, the truth may be somewhere in between.

7 Collins, Jim (2001). *Good to Great.* New York: Harper Business.
   See discussion on the Hedgehog Concept.

8 Buckingham, Marcus & Clifton, Donald O. (2001). *Now, Discover
   Your Strengths.* New York: The Free Press.

Chapter 9

1 Interbrand, Innovation Metrics. "The 100 Top Brands 2006."
   <u>BusinessWeek Online</u>. <http://bwnt.businessweek.com/brand/>
   (Accessed August 2006).

2 <u>BusinessWeek</u> partners with Interbrand to compile an annual list of
   the top brands in the world. The 2006 list is located at:
   < http://bwnt.businessweek.com/brand/2006/>.

[3] Reichheld, Fred (2006). *The Ultimate Question*. Boston: Harvard Business School Publishing.

[4] We are choosing not to provide a more detailed description of this organization based on confidentiality of there being only 10 Fortune 10 firms.

[5] Division is their term, not ours, as we have been using intervision.

[6] I have seen this in my own organization whereby despite having close partnerships with customers – not to mention doing this for a living – many customers will be even more honest and forthcoming with an independent person that I have partnered with.

[7] I have personally experienced this as a former marketing leader of a Fortune 200 company where I thought I "knew" the customers based on discussions with sales and other organizational leaders. Luckily, my leader gave the go-ahead for research, proving me, sales and others to be incorrect in what we thought we knew.

[8] At this time, it is too early to discuss the results as the research was completed in Spring of 2007.

[9] Quantitative research may take the form of an electronic questionnaire, telephone survey or mail questionnaire. As previously mentioned, it typically focuses on numbers such as "rate this on a scale of 1 to 7." This research can be easier to administer, is a lower investment than qualitative, is faster, and can be more confidential and convenient. The collection of information is also quicker. Cons of this approach are less detailed information, less certainty in response rate with mail and electronic venues, and less control over the information received (and from whom). Qualitative research is more direct, such as face-to-face interviews, focus groups, or more open-ended questions. There is generally more control over the responses and response rate; more detailed information vs. numbers; more detailed probing and questions by a good facilitator; and more detailed feelings, attitudes, perceptions and underlying behaviors. Cons include higher investments of time

and money, and it may not provide a complete representative sample as sample sizes may be lower than quantitative research.

Chapter 10

[1] See Graphic 2.1 in Chapter 2.

[2] Reichheld, Fred. "The Right Number of Questions for NPS Surveys." Net Promoter Blog. December 27, 2006.

[3] Customers are asked these items *after* the experience has occurred. If ratings are low, it is probably too late to save this customer; despite being able to learn areas to improve for the future. The areas to improve are why CSI can and should be continued in some manner; however, it is not enough to save customer relationships and partnerships. In addition, it is typically completed with all customers, meaning customers are not prioritized. And when scores are received, what happens next? CSI doesn't provide a method to act upon them. Without a method to act, how can internal touchpoints become involved? The venue this is given is also questionable as it traditionally is completed in one of two ways – a pre-paid postcard given to customers after the experience has occurred or mailed to them either separately or with the invoice ("Here is your invoice, and by the way, please tell us how we did."), or a follow-up phone call is made. In the mail instance, the response rates are always very low. In the call instance, if they receive your voice message, they let you know they called, but don't call you back to speak with you – they expect you to call them (not very friendly).

[4] Jennings, Jason (2002). *Less is More.* New York: The Penguin Group. Almost 60 percent of satisfied customers will leave a company, while 93 percent of completely satisfied customers will remain with a company.

[5] Use your preferred Internet search engine and type in "voice of the customer" and you'll see many descriptions.

[6] While VOC appears to have some system in place to prioritize which customers are involved, it isn't clear what this is. And, as with CSI, the venue this is given is also questionable. Qualitative information alone doesn't provide a complete satisfaction or NPS rating. Another issue with VOC is that, in its traditional format, organizations would speak to customers and ask them about their future needs. The issue arises in that many customers have no idea as to what they will need and/or want next week, next month, or next year. In fact, their expectation is that you – their supplier – should know this, rather than asking them.

[7] Wylie, Ian. "Talk to Our Customers? Are You Crazy?" Fast Company. July/August 2006: 70.

[8] Ibid. The first session is at a customer location and focuses on how to observe customers and what to observe. The second is at another customer location whereby the product or service is used so touchpoints get a feel for it. The third session is at another customer site and customers and/or people (employees) using the product or service are asked a series of questions by the touchpoints. If applicable, a fourth meeting is at the organization's home office, where the touchpoints use the Internet to interact with the product or service for an online experience. Once completed, all information is compiled with recommendations to improve the product or service.

[9] In addition, there isn't an opportunity to prioritize customers as your product can be observed in a variety of venues, although one would hope you would want to observe it in one of your key customer's facilities. Also, while internal touchpoints are involved, it is a select group focused on an entire product or service, rather than a specific customer. Like VOC, it doesn't gain an understanding of complete satisfaction or NPS based on it being a qualitative-only venue. Along with this, the information gained may help an entire product or service line for future growth, yet is not addressing a specific customer's needs. Based on this, we also view Immersion Experience as being reactive – not proactive.

[10] There are many sources of information to learn more about NPS. Two that are suggested are the book, The Ultimate Question by Fred Reichheld: Reichheld, Fred (2006). *The Ultimate Question.* Boston: Harvard Business School Publishing, and <http://www.netpromoter.com/>. Information for this section has been taken from the Internet site (Accessed December 2006).

[11] It may be because it doesn't work with all industries or it doesn't work with small businesses. It is based solely on one quantitative number. One number doesn't tell a complete story about a customer, and more importantly, it doesn't help you decide what to do with the number. And, like CSI, it is <u>reactive</u> – not proactive – as it asks about a customer's experience <u>after</u> it has occurred.

[12] <http://www.netpromoter.com/netpromoter/index.php>. Each of these items is important to the success of any program or process, yet this doesn't resolve the issues with NPS – mainly being reactive and not telling you what to do next. Do you focus on promoters, detractors or passives? What are you supposed to do with them? If you are unable to answer these questions, how can internal touchpoints be involved?

[13] We are choosing not to provide a more detailed description of this organization based on confidentiality of there being only 10 Fortune 10 firms.

[14] Division is their term, not ours, as we have been using intervision.

[15] It is worth noting this Fortune 10 firm also was asking its customers more than the one NPS question, so it appears they also do not feel one question is ultimately enough.

[16] Liker, Jeffrey K. and Thomas Y. Choi. "Building Deep Supplier Relationships." <u>Harvard Business Review</u>. December 2004: 104-113.

Chapter 11

[1] Another consideration for large and mid-sized organizations is which people (roles and titles) to choose for the team. While this varies based on your organizational structure, the intervision representative should be a mid/high-level leader (manager or director) or a next generation leader (an "up and coming" top performer). The former has good knowledge of the area of expertise; the latter provides a great learning and growth experience. When we discuss step 6 about uniting with performance management, the goals of the team become important as these become individual people performance goals as well.

[2] The first question, continue to purchase, provides a measure to determine potential future growth. This is important when creating the action plan. The second question, recommending to others, has been proven to be a good question based on NPS. And the third question, complete satisfaction, relates to the discussion of being satisfied vs. being *completely* satisfied as there is a tremendous difference. For NPS information, see: Reichheld, Fred (2006). *The Ultimate Question*. Boston: Harvard Business School Publishing.

[3] Ibid. We believe NPS is helping achieve consistency with a 1-10 rating scale.

[4] Many other research options only focus on performance. While significant, we believe performance must be correlated with importance and benchmark to be meaningful. Benchmark varies for each organization as it can be described in three ways: (a) It can be defined as the best benchmark supplier your customer partners with, regardless of industry; (b) It can be defined as the best in your industry; and (c) Despite which of the first two is decided, the customer may consider a different benchmark for each attribute. The key is to define how you will use benchmark as part of your initial customer-team discussion and effectively communicate this to customer as part of your AL^2A process.

[5] The first question presents an opportunity for customers to provide other qualitative information that does not relate to an attribute, or to stress a rating related to an attribute. While the second question correlates with one of our previously discussed issues with VOC and the need for an Immersion Experience to observe vs. asking customers that may have no idea of future needs, we have found its inclusion provides for the ability of "delighters."

[6] Our recommended communications steps include: calling the customer lead person, following up with an e-mail or letter, and actually providing all customer touchpoints with the measurement tool you have created. Done in this order enhances the opportunity for complete participation with the customer. A good external partner should draft this communication for you as this demonstrates their alignment with the process, customer team and your organization.

[7] Confidentiality may apply to individual customer touchpoints as they may not want their specific ratings to be seen. An external partner can insure this occurs and analyze all touchpoints' data as one customer vs. individual components (the whole is the same as the sum of its parts). Second, confidentiality may also apply during the qualitative discussion meeting. Again, all information will be analyzed; however, your organization will not know specifically who said what. Benefits of the confidentiality are obtaining more open and honest quantitative responses, as well as achieving an open and honest qualitative discussion.

[8] See Chapter 11 Customers In Action for large, mid-sized and small organizations.

[9] This presents a combination of previously discussed elements such as CSI, VOC, Immersion Experience and NPS. The quantitative nature of CSI and NPS are incorporated and expanded through AL^2A through the quantitative measurement tool and its inclusion of qualitative open-ended questions, which improve VOC. Also, the discovery session integrates and enhances VOC and Immersion Experience through a more detailed qualitative process and integration of internal touchpoints via the customer-specific team.

It is recommended to do the discovery session face-to-face for a more personal approach; however, it can be done via telephone conference. Ideally, all customer touchpoints attend one meeting to have all of their input and discussion at once vs. separate one-on-one meetings. The use and benefits of an external partner to facilitate this meeting have already been discussed.

[10] It is good not to reveal the ratings until the face-to-face meeting, to avoid any preconceived notions. This makes it vital to have all members of the customer team available at the meeting to foster conversation about key issues. Having all customer touchpoints at the meeting together presents several benefits. As items are discussed, it provides the customer with an opportunity and venue to openly communicate issues. Doing so can help solve their own internal issues. It also gets them aligned regarding overall issues and opportunities to grow the partnership. Oftentimes, the finance person only interacts with your finance person and isn't aware of what else occurs within the business. Also, the discovery session presents an opportunity to educate more customer touchpoints about your organization, as well as its own, creating more promoters and evangelists.

[11] Requests range from customer requests for more consistent updates to reduced transit times. Discussions you have had in the past are irrelevant; this is a chance to develop an action plan to completely satisfy this customer. One example may be the customer requests a three day deliver time. Distribution says this is not possible, yet we know anything is possible – for a price. This may go into the plan with an explanation of the investment needed for it. The customer can then determine it may no longer be important.

[12] An example of some items in a draft action plan (not in SMART format) includes: (a) Verbatim comments such as, "Jill is very knowledgeable and serves us well." "Tom always has issues with responding quickly to our requests." "Marketing needs to have more autonomy to make decisions." (b) Company X needs to improve responsiveness in all areas as everything takes too much time and effort. Their corporate headquarters is slow to respond and they need better processes to change this. (c) Company X

needs to be more innovative with new product development. We expect this from them if they want to continue to do business with us. (d) Our freight costs are too high. Can Company X consolidate shipments with anyone else to reduce our costs? (e) We would like to go on a site tour at least four times per year.

[13] Part of the final customer action plan is to incorporate delighters, if applicable. Delighters should not be included with the draft action plan. As they are delighters, they are meant to delight customers, which is why they should only be included with the final action plan. They present an additional "wow" factor for the customer. Once completed, either the entire customer-specific team or a few key team members should schedule a meeting to present to the customer. All participating customer touchpoints should be included so they all see the finished action plan.

[14] As a general rule, we have found creation and approval of the draft action plan should take a minimum of one week and a maximum of three weeks. Approval of the final action plan is an additional one to three weeks. And execution begins immediately and should be planned for one year as the process should be conducted annually.

[15] Organizations wanting to do measurement with all customers can use the measurement tool to accomplish this as it provides quick and easy ratings of several key attributes and the Value Index offers one simple number.

Epilogue

[1] <http://www.metrics2.com/blog/business_metrics/dealsma/>

[2] Becker, Matthias M., Bogardus, Anna J. & Oldham, Timothy. "Mastering revenue growth in M&A." The McKinsey Quarterly. June 2001.

[3] Prior to a letter of intent being signed, there is a comprehensive process – relating to Strategy – of target selection. The strategy behind an acquisition process begins with a sub-process of

determining which organizations are contained on your target
selection list. As discussions begin with the target selections, a
letter of intent may be signed to begin the due diligence process.

[4] Our assumption is the reader has a basic level of understanding and
knowledge of an acquisition and integration process.

[5] The integration leader should be selected as early as possible in the
process and should be part of the due diligence team, as if the
acquisition becomes an integration, this individual needs to have
all possible information. Being involved early prevents duplication
of information and/or lost information if the individual joins too
late in the process, or once the deal is officially signed.

[6] This is not an all exhaustive due diligence list as there are several
other items that could be included. Onsite rules may not seem
necessary; however, we have experienced instances where this did
not occur and members of the due diligence team actually went
onsite to the target company wearing logo shirts of their own
company. This did not create a high sense of confidentially and
caused many problems.

[7] The assumption is that an organization is doing some type of
integration, although this doesn't have to be complete integration
of all systems, etc. Based on an article by Richard Ettenson and
Jonathan Knowles, companies continue to exist independently in
almost 24 percent of acquisitions. See Ettenson, Richard and
Jonathan Knowles. "Merging the Brands and Branding the
Merger." MIT Sloan Management Review. Summer 2006: 39-49.

[8] In Section I, we mentioned the puzzle piece of strategy contains
areas such as operations, technology, manufacturing, financials,
etc.

[9] Much of determining the right customers should be accomplished
during due diligence as once the deal is signed, it is too late to
discover if these are the wrong customers, impacting the success
and financial objectives of the integration.

[10] Our intent is not to delve into specifics of what to do during an integration. Following the Strategy, People, Customers model, we want to demonstrate how each puzzle piece can and should be applied to any core organizational process. In our experiences, an acquisition and integration represents a comprehensive example of this application.

[11] As with the overall integration and the customer strategy, our intent is not to delve into specifics of what to do with people during an integration. The cultural assessment and communication, as well as all other people strategy elements contain extensive time and effort to achieve success. As previously mentioned, we have found the technology-based integration system to be of great assistance.

Bibliography

Becker, Matthias M., Bogardus, Anna J. & Oldham, Timothy. "Mastering revenue growth in M&A." The McKinsey Quarterly. June 2001.

Bliss, William. G. "Cost of Employee Turnover." The Advisor. 2006. <http://www.isquare.com/turnover.cfm> (Accessed July 2006).

Brown, Dan (2003). *The Da Vinci Code*. New York: Doubleday.

Buckingham, Marcus & Clifton, Donald O. (2001). *Now, Discover Your Strengths*. New York: The Free Press.

BusinessWeek partners with Interbrand to compile an annual list of the top brands in the world. The 2006 list is located at: < http://bwnt.businessweek.com/brand/2006/>.

Choi, Thomas Y., & Liker, Jeffrey K. "Building Deep Supplier Relationships." Harvard Business Review. December 2004: 104-113.

Collins, Jim (2001). *Good to Great*. New York: Harper Business.

Conlin, Michelle. "Champions of Innovation." BusinessWeek: Inside Innovation. June 2006: 18-26.

Cook, Kevin. "The Greatest Show in Sports: SportsCenter." Playboy: January 2007: 60.

Daniel, Teresa A., J.D. & Metcalf, Gary S., PhD. "The Fundamentals of Employee Recognition." May 2005. Society of Human Resources Management: White Paper.

Ettenson, Richard & Knowles, Jonathan. "Merging the Brands and Branding the Merger." MIT Sloan Management Review. Summer 2006: 39-49.

Finigan, Kathleen. "Setting Specific Goals Improves an Employee's Performance." The Business Review. June 1998. <http://albany.bizjournals.com/albany/stories/1998/06/08/smallb3.html?page=2> (Accessed February 2007)

Fishman, Charles. "Wal-Mart You Don't Know." Fast Company December 2003. <www.fastcompany.com> (Accessed August 2006).

Fleming, John, H., Coffman, Curt & Harter, James K. "Manage Your Human Sigma." Harvard Business Review. July-August 2005: 107-114.

Franzke, Brandon. "Fuel Injection." Illumin. Volume 2: Issue iii. March 1, 2002. University of Southern California Viterbi School of Engineering. <http://illumin.usc.edu> (Accessed March 2007).

Garsten, Ed. "Cadillac Spins New Sales With Branded Bicycles." The Detroit News. July 2006. <http://www.detnews.com/2005/autosinsider/0507/26/C01-258961.htm> (Accessed February 2007).

Grensin-Pophal, Linda. "Follow Me." HR Magazine. February 2000: Vol. 45, No. 2: 36-41.

<http://www.metrics2.com/blog/business_metrics/dealsma/>

<http://www.netpromoter.com/netpromoter/index.php>. We are choosing not to provide a more detailed description of this organization based on confidentiality of there being only 10 Fortune 10 firms.

Huselid, Mark A., Beatty, Richard W. & Becker, Brian E. "A Players or Positions?" Harvard Business Review. December 2005: 110-117.

Interbrand, Innovation Metrics. "The 100 Top Brands 2006." BusinessWeek Online. <http://bwnt.businessweek.com/brand/> (Accessed August 2006).

Jennings, Jason (2002). *Less is More.* New York: The Penguin Group.

Kelley, Thomas. "The Ten Faces of Innovation." Manufacturing Matters! Conference. Midwest Airlines Center, Milwaukee, May 15, 2006.

Liker, Jeffrey K. and Thomas Y. Choi. "Building Deep Supplier Relationships." Harvard Business Review. December 2004: 104-113.

Lockwood, Nancy R. "Leveraging Employee Engagement for Competitive Advantage: HR's Strategic Role." 2007 SHRM Research Quarterly.

Mankins, Michael C. & Steele, Richard. "Stop Making Plans Start Making Decisions." Harvard Business Review. January 2006: 76-84.

McConnell, Beth. "Employee Loyalty, Engagement Grow Same Qualities in Customers." Society for Human Resource Management. September 2005. <http://www.shrm.org/hrnews_published/archives/CMS_014189.asp> (Accessed May 2006).

Ohno, Taiichi (1988). *Toyota Production Systems – Beyond Large-Scale Production.* New York: Productivity Press.

Reichheld, Fred. "The Right Number of Questions for NPS Surveys." Net Promoter Blog. December 27, 2006.

Reichheld, Fred (2006). *The Ultimate Question.* Boston: Harvard Business School Publishing.

Thackray, John. "Feedback for Real." Gallup Management Journal. March 2001: <http://gmj.gallup.com/content/default.aspx?ci=811> (Accessed July 2006).

Williams, David H. "The Strategic Implications of Wal-Mart's RFID
Mandate." <u>Directions Magazine</u>. July 29, 2004.
<<u>http://www.directionsmag.com/article.php?article_id=629&trv=1</u>
>. (Accessed August 2006).

Wylie, Ian. "Talk to Our Customers? Are You Crazy?" <u>Fast
Company</u>. July/August 2006: 70.

About the Author

With a passion to help others become more productive and successful, David Yeghiaian (pronounced Yeg – E – I – an) formed Unique Business Solutions in April 2004. Unique Business Solutions are strategic business advisors that partner with high-performing businesses on issues strategy, people and customers to help them maximize their productivity and profitability.

With more than 15 years of experience, David has demonstrated results on a global scale in a breadth of organizational services such as marketing communications, acquisitions and integrations, brand management, strategic planning and process excellence. His experience includes work with Fortune 500, non-profit, government and private organizations around the world. He is a successful change agent who works to increase market share and lower costs, maximize profitability, and continuously improve organizations.

Prior to forming Unique Business Solutions, David worked at global companies such as Rockwell Automation, the Falk Corporation (at the time a subsidiary of United Technologies Corporation), and Schreiber Foods; as well as the Wisconsin Department of Transportation.

A strong believer in continuous learning, David is an adjunct instructor at the University of Wisconsin-Green Bay, having previously taught courses on corporate strategy, business, leadership, marketing and communications. He previously taught at Cardinal Stritch University and Lakeland College.

David has spoke at several conferences on topics related to Strategy, People and Customers; as well as topics regarding any specific section or chapter of this book (i.e., strategic planning, AL^2A with People, AL^2A with Customers, strategic marketing, performance management, brand management, customer strategy, acquisitions and integrations, etc.). He is a member of the American Marketing Association (AMA) and Society of Human Resource Professionals (SHRM).

Community involvement is important to David, as he is involved in and supports many activities. He is a Board member of the Rotary Club of Green Bay; and New North Inc., an 18-county economic development effort. He also is Chair of the New North's Small Business & Entrepreneurial Council, and former Board member of the Green Bay Chamber of Commerce's Advance Board for Economic Development and various symphony orchestra boards. He earned a Bachelor of Arts from Marquette University and a Master of Arts from Concordia University.

David and his wife Kim were born and raised in Milwaukee, and have resided in Green Bay, Wisconsin since 2002.

He is available to speak to organizations, leadership summits, team building sessions, and other venues. If you ever attend one of his presentations, please introduce yourself. He enjoys meeting people and learning what you've experienced.

Feel free to contact David at **info@unique-solutionsinc.com**, or more information can be accessed at **www.strategypeoplecustomers.com** or **www.unique-solutionsinc.com**.